Journey Through the World of Spirit
God, Gaia, and Guardian Angels

by David L. Oakford

Foreword by John Jay Harper
Author of Tranceformers: Shamans of the 21st Century

Reality Press
An imprint of Reality Entertainment, Inc.

For information contact:

REALITY ENTERTAINMENT
P.O. Box 91
Foresthill, CA 95631

ph: 530-367-5389, fx: 530-367-3024

www.reality-entertainment.com

ISBN: 0-9791750-9-7
Printed in the United States of America

Book Cover Artwork © Robert Sharen, 2007

Contents

v

Acknowledgments

First and foremost, I want to thank everyone who inspired me to write my book *Journey Through the World of Spirit*. Specifically, my wife and family who encouraged as well as put up with me as I went through these decisions on how to present my visions of the Spirit World that surrounds this one completely. In fact, without their support, I wouldn't have shared my NDE story in the first place, period. I do not seek fortune or fame; I only want the truth to be known: We do not die!

Second, I also wish to express my appreciation to Kevin Williams for placing my NDE story on www.near-death.com and to Lilo Kinne: www.lilokinne.com. Without their help, my little story would still be my little secret. Equally, I thank all the people who wrote me with their questions after reading the profile of my story on the Internet. These particular people were, and still are, instrumental in helping me process the metaphysical event that changed my perception of life, death and the hereafter, and place it all into a larger context.

Third, I also thank the folks I met in the on-line metaphysics "chat rooms" for listening to and bearing with my several sporadic attempts to tell the story in the early days. My book is dedicated to all of you now as well. I'd name all of you here one-by-one, in fact, but you know who you are and I respect your request for anonymity. There are a few of you, however, that I do wish to single out: Especially Animus Kid, Gee Purz, Vana, Swannie and Hirophant Prime. Indeed, I am honored to have known you all and hope that you are enjoying your customized version of the afterlife. We will meet again!

Finally, I am grateful to Warren Croyle, CEO, Reality Entertainment, and John Jay Harper, Editor-in-Chief, Reality Press, for bringing my true story to this larger worldwide audience via www.reality-entertainment.com. Likewise I am blessed to have PMH Atwater's endorsement for my book too. No doubt, Dr. Atwater probably knows more about the near-death experience in general than anyone. I'm grateful she is around to help people like me who need to process what happened to them and contend with the aftereffects that a (NDE) creates in us.

Foreword

God, Gaia, and Guardian Angels

Once in awhile I come across a manuscript that grabs me by my heart instead of by my head. And this is one of those stories before you now.

Much like a beloved poem or a song, the words do not have to be complex but rather they have to hit a resonant chord within and give meaning to our existence on earth. This does that in triplicate, offering an array of facts and deep-seated insights into the living beings we call God, Gaia, and Guardian Angels.

Yet, there is more to this book than warm and fuzzy feel-good platitudes; it has teeth. I mean it chews away at you until you finally realize that David Oakford had one of the most profound near-death experiences ever brought to the public's awareness today.

Clearly, this is a story that will bless millions of people on a planet that is in the throes of chaos in climate and consciousness—and one day we will realize they are forever linked together. This is the type of tale that indeed needs to be told on The Oprah Winfrey Show.

John Jay Harper
Author of *Tranceformers: Shamans of the 21st Century*

www.johnjayharper.com and www.reality-entertainment.com

Preface

My name is David and I have a story to share with you that changed my life for the worst—and the better. For this is an experience I've kept to myself since 1979 with the exception that I did write a draft of this book in 1998 after I found the Internet to be a relatively safe place to tell the story to other people.

You see, for the most part I was afraid to tell anyone what happened to me for fear of being labeled a crazy man. Indeed, that is what our human species does well; it seeks to eliminate nonconformists. In fact, I tried really hard to forget the whole thing myself because it was just too weird and I didn't have anything I could compare it to then or now.

I didn't have anyone to talk to about it either.

So I've been carrying my NDE story around inside of me as a tight-knot in my gut for nearly 30 years. This strain has affected my life in many ways, some positive, but some very negative. And any person that has been through psychotherapy will tell you that it helps to get things off your chest, as well as your stomach. But I was clinically depressed before the near-death experience (NDE) and even more so afterward.

Thus, in order to tell my story to the public, I needed to heal from its trauma as well as mature from its insights. Since my otherworldly experience didn't magically remove my problems, I still had much growing to do in my life.

There was no "divine" intervention that took away the alcohol and drug abuse issues that I had then. Indeed I've spent decades since my NDE addressing those issues, and as we say in all the 12-Step programs that is a job best-handled one day at a time.

Albeit upon hindsight, I realize that I was being prepared to write this book in the summer of 1997 after I read James Redfield's *The Celestine Prophesy*. Immediately I recognized the insights presented in it were familiar to me. I knew that life, death, and rebirth were about the use, abuse, and recycling of life force energies.

This prompted me to consider what I was doing with my own gift of energy, in particular, because I was an extremely negative, unhappy person. I was not satisfied with my life events at all; I was dangerously close to just giving up on the whole thing.

I strongly regretted returning to this planet and wanted to just go back to my Home in Heaven—and stay there. As I assessed my situation, it was either give up and succumb to being a negative person, or consider being a positive one for a change of pace, to see what would happen.

No doubt I was at the crossroads of crisis and opportunity, as the Chinese sages put it. It was as if I were being forced to find a new way of living as an immortal being of energy. Lao Tsu, author of the *Tao Te Ching*—Book of Changes—had it right: "Being at one with the Tao is eternal, though the body dies, the Tao will never pass away." (Verse 16)

In truth, our task is to live with the Tao, the way things are, but as if still flying-free in heaven while firmly-grounded by life's daily burdens on Earth. The trick is to stay upbeat as we are beat down. Yet being a positive person wasn't an easy thing for me. I looked at life from the proverbial "cup half-empty" point of view.

Nonetheless, the insights in *The Celestine Prophesy* spurred me into choosing to process my experience from a positive point of view overall. Equally, I discovered that I could use what I learned in my NDE - specifically how energy is circulated through creation and us - to benefit all that I came in contact with.

Using my life energy wisely was the key to awakening further.

Ultimately I overcame my reservations, I began to talk with people about what happened to me and share the visions that I knew were of great value to mankind just as John Jay Harper shared in his book *Tranceformers: Shamans of the 21st Century:*

By illustration, I think this is precisely what happens to the person who has a near-death experience (NDE). They find themselves surrounded by an overwhelming display of information, past, present, and future lifetimes surface in a whole life review that looks at us from its largest perspective—Top Down. Yet there is a larger purpose: This scene is carefully choreographed, designed to show us what we have created up to that point in time and that hurts like hell as a rule!

That is, we see and *feel the impact* we have on each other and our planet through our stinking negative thinking and heartless actions. Specifically, we learn that our belief system has shaped itself into our experience of life. We reap exactly what we've sown … in others!

In other words, we see how we reflect, "mirror" or stack up—or not—to the love story that was in fact God's own version of the ideal man: Jesus. (Of course, when I use the term "man" I am not being a sexist; so relax about it.)

Moreover, I am of the opinion that there is more to this old, old story as well. I recall an incident where a woman saw Jesus immediately upon her near-death event. He began speaking to her in an Old Elizabethan Bible English style of "Thee and "Thou," upon which this lady informed this "outdated" Jesus: "We don't talk like that anymore." In essence, get with the program. Jesus then simply smiled at her and vanished.

To the point: Is it not high time for us to pull our head out of our past, grow up and take self-responsibility for our actions? Do we want to stay as children, victims of our self-made circumstances, or learn how to overcome them through calling upon the power of the Christ within us? Apostle Paul said as much: "Christ in you, the hope of glory!"

Dr. Harper knows, as I do from my NDE, Jesus is a Master Teacher, the supreme example for us to emulate. He showed that life and death challenges brought on by heartless acts of others can be faced with compassion and grace with God's help.

But I wasn't a teacher, or a preacher; I was just a teenage kid then and I couldn't walk up to strangers on the street and tell them: "Jesus Loves You!" No one was going to listen to that message from a misfit other than to offer me a free ride to a psychiatric hospital!

Thus, I needed a safe place—a neutral space—where I could share my insights and then walk away if I became uncomfortable. I discovered these Internet chat rooms might work, so I explored a few of them. It was nice; nobody had to know my real name and I could just click the little red "x" box in the upper right-hand corner of my computer screen to exit if I got too scared to proceed.

Ultimately I found a safe chat room where the topic was metaphysics and the participants were also enjoying themselves sharing this information. I, of course, realized that what had happened to me qualified as a "meta," a "beyond," the physical event and these folks were extremely interested in hearing my firsthand insights into how the people and planet worked with energy—vibrations.

Eventually, a chat acquaintance from the United Kingdom asked me to write a short essay telling him what had happened to me during my NDE. This, therefore, was my first attempt to formally write down my *Journey Through the World of Spirit*. That small, easy-to-read essay version later found its way to Kevin Williams and www.near-death.com and is featured there in that large database of NDEs.

Soon I began receiving emails from all over the world, people thanking me for writing the story in such a simple way and sharing my vision of life after death. That initial encouragement inspired me to sit down and more carefully record the entire NDE episode today because I know my story has helped a lot of people.

This realization is rewarding in and of itself.

I sensed most of these folks simply wanted to understand what happens to us when we die. By sharing my NDE, I was making a positive difference in their lives, if no one else's at that time. This made me feel good inside and valuable to the scheme of life.

This was important; *not* to have people dismiss my story as "only" a bad drug trip. It was so much more than that implies: hallucination, illusion. The drugs were the catalysts to blast the true "me" out-of-my-body, nothing else!

However, I used that same excuse to keep my NDE tightly-locked away for 30 years; though to be honest, that never did work well for me. These insights would leak out now and again in the most unexpected as well as untimely ways.

Yet, in the end, my story is what it is, I finally realized, a true story containing useful information that one can choose to use in their own daily life interactions with others for positive life-enhancing purposes—or not.

Thus, if you don't believe my NDE that is your choice, you have free-will, and I understand that you are exercising it. I didn't want to believe it either for a long, long time, until I had to accept that we are in fact all in this world to work together like bees in a hive in order to bring heaven to earth.

No man is an island after all.

Chapter 1

How This Happened

"By three methods we may learn wisdom:
First, by reflection, which is noblest;
second, by imitation, which is easiest;
and third by experience, which is the bitterest."
—*Confucius*

Before I go forward, I want this point to be made crystal-clear to my readers, critics or believers: I'm not a religious person. Nor am I a psychic, a guru, a therapist, or anything other than a husband and father to four children.

My college degree is in accounting and I live a life that probably isn't all that much different from your own. In plain terms, I still have to deal with the day-to-day grind to make the car and house payments. I still toil to keep the lights on and put food on the table.

More so, I don't have a self-help regimen for you to follow, or a class to teach, or a seminar to give. But I do offer, for what it's worth, a book full-of-wisdom that I rediscovered in my *Journey Through The World of Spirit*.

Specifically, in the spring of 1979 I overdosed on the drug known as PCP, died, and was shown around our solar system by a being made of light that I call "Bob." That aspect of my story in and of itself usually gets a smile and a hearty laugh at a minimum.

Yes, I did drugs then but that did not distort the meaning or the vision of what I experienced; rather it merely opened the gateway of consciousness to it. So I am not going to apologize for my behavior or make excuses for it, or cover it up in any way, shape, or form.

To be blunt, I was nineteen years old and a loser.

That is, I started smoking cigarettes when I was 13, marijuana, or "pot" when I was 15. I likewise began drinking beer around the same time. I, of course, had no car or driver's license, no job, no girlfriend. I could go on and on here as to what I didn't have including a strong will to survive, but you get the idea; I simply had no life as I know it today.

So by age nineteen, I was getting high on a daily basis as I was an extremely depressed young man. And although I thought my life should be better than it was, like others in a similar boat that was sinking fast, I didn't do anything to make it better and help save myself.

Later on I knew that I wouldn't get anywhere unless I decided to change my ways, so I actually devised a plan to escape from the drugs, drinking, and everything else that I felt was dragging me down and causing me to be so dysfunctional.

This desire for self-improvement led me to save money in order to leave town in the spring. Indeed I saved a few thousand dollars so I would be able to survive on my own terms for awhile. I figured out that if I was all by myself and on the road, I'd be able to make good choices, ones that wouldn't be influenced by people who were themselves making the same bad choices I was at that time.

I wouldn't have any friends to party with nor would I know who to see to get drugs once I left town. I'd be free of these other losers once and for all.

I'd been to the Southwest United States when I was thirteen, and I decided to go there again. This was going to be the ultimate great escape from reality. I had all the camping equipment, money, and skills needed to live in the wilderness I reasoned.

Equally, I'd done my share of "fighting" for sobriety and that didn't get me anywhere, so now I was scared enough to try the "flight" option.

Albeit I wanted to attend one final party as a farewell celebration, with my so-called friends, before I left town. In my mind, one more time wouldn't hurt anything and as destiny would have it, one of my friend's hippie-type parents happened to be on a cruise ship.

It was always nice to find a house party going on just as the weather turned warmer in southeastern Michigan. This home was one of the smaller single story brick-types in Warren—my hometown. I lived in a lower middle class neighborhood in the shadow of the automobile factories. The houses here were mostly small, but this one had a large addition that was all fixed up as the ultimate party room.

I'm serious; there was a pool table, a bar, and an extremely powerful stereo sound system. There were several very inviting chairs and plenty of floor space for dancing—and crashing!

My friends and I started drinking beer and smoking pot early on this warm and wonderful mid-June afternoon and it was a magical day for sure. School was out for the summer, and it was time to party; play, swim, and sleep outside in comfort.

Toward that evening, I decided I wanted to liven up the party a bit. After all, this was the last one I wanted to attend with my friends now. So I wanted it to be memorable and feel special and I turned to what we called "Smoking T." We used to put this drug into joints to spice them up, increase the effect of euphoria.

A friend came over, and sold me what I thought was a packet of Smoking T. It didn't look like the same stuff I was used to however. It was a yellowish-brown color, and looked like a crystallized rock of some sorts. I figured this drug was in an uncut form and just needed to be crushed up to be smoked.

Nonetheless, my friend did warn me to leave the stuff alone until he came back. He said it wasn't the normal substance I was used to from previous parties; but I didn't listen to his warning and that was a mistake.

Indeed I thought he was just trying to rip me off, so I took the rock out, crushed most of it up, snorted some, and rolled the rest into joints. When my friend returned, he smelled what we were smoking and asked what I did with the new drug?

I told him I snorted it.

He looked stunned; then said this was PCP and that I would be lucky to be alive tomorrow. He warned me again but yet I refused to believe him because I was an experienced drug taker. I had the "invincible teen" thing going. I was confident I would handle this problem, and live to tell about it. My friend didn't believe me, but I was determined not to look scared in front of everyone.

After our chat, we all went on the patio outside to drink more beer and enjoy the approaching twilight. I could see my parents sitting on their porch across the street. They were about fifty yards away but I didn't think they could see me. I thought this is funny: I was there, higher than a kite and they were right there with no idea where I was, what I was doing, or even what I was planning to do, leave them for good!

Although I was higher than I ever felt in my life, I also felt happy too. I was looking forward to going off to "make it" in the world. I had this sense of being really alive and totally rejected the idea that I was about to face an overwhelming, life or death, medical crisis.

Unfortunately, my sense of invincibility started to evaporate right before—and behind—my eyes. Initially, I was having trouble maintaining my balance, and choices were narrow: either sit down now under my own power—or fall down.

Soon even sitting there on the cement porch steps of the patio wasn't working either. I started to get scared when my dizziness increased to an intolerable degree.

Suddenly it hit me: I was going to pass out cold!

Indeed I knew what that felt like too because I'd been rendered unconscious several times. In particular, I was hit in the head with a baseball bat and I was feeling that way again. Instinctively, an awful feeling of dread surfaced to the top of my mind: I was in deep, deep trouble.

I panicked.

I quickly lowered myself down to the ground; I wanted to lie on the soft green grass, feel the earth underneath my body in one last desperate effort to remain conscious. The spinning stopped, eventually, but then I faded slowly but surely into unconsciousness. I was a leaf blowing in the wind, I mused, simply drifting, drifting, drifting into a peaceful blackness.

Chapter 2

The Initial Out of Body Experience

"At the moment of death the sum of all the experiences of life on earth comes to the surface of the mind—for in the mind are stored all the impressions of past deeds and the dying man then becomes absorbed in these experiences."
—Bhagavad-Gita

The next thing I remember I was sitting in a friend's 1974 sky blue Chevy Impala 4-door speeding down the road with my buddies sitting all around me chatting away. I also tried to talk to them, but I was only receiving bits and pieces of what they were saying, in fact, as if we were out-of-synch with each other.

They couldn't hear or see me at all—like I was *invisible*?

We rode around the block, passing directly in front of my childhood home several times. I remember seeing my parents sitting on their porch and I ducked down in the seat. I knew if they saw me they would know I was high and they would surely punish me for it. After we passed by my folks, we turned east down Ten Mile Road toward the power-line transmission easement. As we crossed it, the surroundings looked like northern Michigan. Then it dawned on me, my friends had cruised way up north, crossed the Mackinac Bridge, turned around, and were now on the way back to Metro Detroit again.

As we traveled along the highway, I started "feeling" our world in a whole new way; as a part of me. It was as if I was an extension of the Earth. That sensation was strange indeed; to feel at one with the total environment.

There was something missing in this landscape, too. I could tell that much, but I was not sure exactly what was absent or what that really even meant then. I later learned that cities were low energy regions caused by the paving over of the green ground cover, destruction of animal and plant habitats, and the mismanagement of renewable natural resources overall by human beings who were greedy and ignorant.

Whatever the case, I was very attracted to the trees.

I felt their strength, and I could both see and feel that their roots reached deep into the ground. I sensed how they were able to connect with and contribute to the planet as much as or more than what they took away from it in nutrients.

Moreover, I was awestruck because they were able to withstand the changes of the seasons and in spite of the destructive influences of humans in general they still survived. I respected the trees that remained alive and thriving because so many of them were bulldozed down to make room for the asphalt suburbs of Motown.

Here is an interesting observation: I saw some little fairylike beings in and around every tree. They looked like the elves one might see in fairy tale books. They were male, female, young and old, and were as diverse in appearance and demeanor as humans are today. When I looked directly at them, they sensed it because they quickly turned away to melt back into the tree leaves. If I turned my head to look directly at them, they would be gone in a flash, without a trace.

There was one being who didn't turn away however.

He looked directly into my eyes and gave me a huge smile, scoring a direct hit to my heart. He was about a foot tall, much bigger and older than the other ones of his kind with bright-colored clothing on, but most importantly was the fact that he loved me! In fact, he was living in a tree that I used to climb as a child. I watched him as we drove down the street wondering to myself: why didn't he vanish when I looked at him like his peers had done?

At any rate, I blacked-out again.

Chapter 3

An Awakening

"In three words I can sum up everything about life; it goes on."
—Robert Frost

Then I woke-up in the black Lazy Boy lounge chair that my friends evidently had put me in late that evening. I still saw the stocked bar, stereo system, shag carpet on the floor, and the paneled walls in the room. There was a door on the north side and a few small windows as well. However, I didn't see any of my friends standing or sitting around me now.

Everything looked normal but I didn't feel normal; I could actually feel the organs in my body working! I could direct my focus to each of my organ systems and feel their individual vibrations separately, or enjoy all of them working together in harmony as a single vibration with overtones like an orchestra playing a song in tune.

Specifically, I could plainly hear and feel my heart steadily beating away like a drum and thoroughly enjoyed the feel of my blood rushing throughout my entire body. In fact, I could identify the sounds that all of the organs and glands made.

All of them resounding together made a strange, eerie, albeit familiar song of sorts that I cannot describe in a few words. It was a buzz, a hum, and I must say that it had a wonderful harmony that rang true, felt normal to me, not foreign. It was like a symphony that I'd never heard before, but paradoxically, somehow, I knew every single note of it – dare I say – by heart!

No matter, these sweet musical notes turned sour in a few minutes, and my awe turned into deep shock as my organs began to shut down!

Initially, I felt my glands slowing down. As each of them slowed in vibration their contribution to the beautiful symphony slowed as well. Eventually their secretions stopped altogether and their parts in the song weren't replaced: They fell silent.

Next were the major organs.

Like my glands, the rest of my organs slowed and stopped, with my heart going last. I literally heard my heart stop and felt my blood stop moving. There was a silence that stunned; I didn't know what to think at all other than I remembered what my friend had told me about doing enough of the drug to kill me.

But I was still conscious of what I was feeling and thinking and everything made perfect sense to me thus far. So I reasoned that I could not be dead, could I?

In fact, if what I had heard about God from the teachings of churches were true, if I were dead, then I'd see a devil, be cast into the pits of hell, or maybe even see an angel and be taken to heaven depending on my lifestyle. Yet I saw no darkness, no pits of fire, nor no pearly gates either for that matter. Everything still looked pretty normal, at least for those first few extremely quiet moments.

Then suddenly I was aware that the stereo was playing songs from "*The Doors,*" but with the volume way too loud for comfort! Nonetheless, I didn't care because I thought that if I heard the stereo playing, then surely I was not dead, right?

Anyway, I felt revived.

Yet the stereo was too loud, even for me. As a rule, I liked loud rock music and wondered why all of a sudden this song bothered me? This song seemed more like noise and that was the irritant; it was no longer in harmony with my organs' natural song. It was as if the sound I heard coming from my body was uniquely right for me, and the other music I was hearing was very out of tune, increasingly obnoxious and even dangerous in some unexplainable way.

Now I couldn't see my friends, so I wanted to search for them, but, oddly enough, I didn't have to physically move anywhere. I could see into the other rooms of the house at once just by wondering to myself what might be in them. That new ability was a bit bizarre for certain.

Although I confess, this new skill seemed totally natural to me and I didn't question it at all at that time. Completing my scan, I found the entire house to be completely empty; I was indeed home alone. Since no one was in the house I got up from my chair to turn the music down myself, but I couldn't do it.

The volume control did not move as I tried to turn it nor was I able to unplug the stupid thing from the wall. No matter what motion I went through then, in fact, the music kept playing louder and louder and louder. It felt like this intolerable noise was slicing through me like a sharp knife. This disturbance, finally, led me to acknowledge that there was something terribly wrong going on here, even though I couldn't figure it out.

Clearly I was confused and I needed help. I called out for my friends but nobody came to my rescue. I tried once again to unplug the stereo but that still didn't work either because I could not grasp the cord with my hand. The stereo just kept playing this unnerving screech that was rattling the core of my being.

My discomfort grew and I couldn't stop it. It was like I had no sense of touch with this world. I tried to convince myself it must be the effects of the drug and it would wear off in time. Maybe, I mused, I too was tuned to a new channel of existence?

Whatever the case, I still needed to do something about the noise that was growing exponentially louder. I mentally ran all over the house calling for my friends, shrieking that the music was too freaking loud. I resorted to begging and crying for the music to be turned down. I tried to go outside to escape the noise but since I could not feel the doorknob, I couldn't turn it. That was when I became overtly frightened, panic set in, as I realized I had absolutely no idea what to do.

I was so, so terrified!

For I could see the sunlight shining through the windows but couldn't get outside to enjoy the beauty of the approaching twilight. I couldn't work the locks and was stumped. Again I peered out the window and now it did look very odd to me. Everything was more detailed than normal and I could see the colors around things glowing like an animated, electrified pastel painting of the landscape. Thus my fear transformed into curiosity as I really wanted to go out there and explore this colorful new world, but I didn't know how to get there and that was annoying.

My body sure wasn't working as it used to do!

The simple things in life like opening doors and windows and operating equipment were beyond my physical capabilities at this point. Ultimately I went to hide in the bathroom in an unsuccessful attempt to escape the noise.

For some reason—habit I guess—I wanted to use the toilet, but I couldn't make my muscles work at all. I tried to wash my face and the faucet would not turn on the flow of water. Like everything else, nothing was responding. I couldn't even pick up a towel so I could use it to muffle the music that seemed to be crawling toward me through the bottom of the door! Talk about a "bad trip."

Worse, I looked in the mirror and I couldn't see myself!

Now I really started to panic. I roamed around the house, crying like a baby and calling for my friends to help me, please; but nobody answered me or came to help.

In fact, moving became a lot harder to do too. Have you ever tried to run in a dream yet not get anywhere? That is exactly how moving about in this dreamlike "space" felt to me then as well.

Somehow I found my way back into the family room only to see my "real" physical body still sitting in the chair! I was sleeping or that is how it looked anyway. But I wondered, how in the world could I be seeing myself? In a way, I was kind of glad to see me there, but really how could I be in two places at the same time?

It was so very, very strange to witness.

This scene made me more frightened because I saw "me" from all different angles except from the inside angle I was used to seeing myself. All I had to do was *think* of the view I wanted to see and my view changed to the one I thought of instantly.

Most troubling was that I didn't like how I looked from the outside perspective. I looked ugly and I could tell there was something missing from my body. Intuitively I felt that what was missing was the true "me"—the conscious awareness that I was now using to see, feel, and reflect upon my body lying lifeless in that lounge chair!

This much was clear: I was alone, confused, and petrified by this existential crisis, a living nightmare unlike any other. I was experiencing up close and personal how much we like to be in control of our environment. Desperate to get my old reality restored, I tried to get back into my body by sitting on it a few times but couldn't connect with it. My body seemed every bit as untouchable as everything else around me.

For that matter, I wasn't touching the floor either.

I was floating around the home. So I willed myself to rise up into the space just above and to the left of my body. I just hung out there for awhile reflecting on my situation, as I could no longer run, walk, or crawl evidently, as I used to do.

Exasperated, I screamed out for help again, but nobody came. Thus I decided to float to the door, and like before I couldn't work the doorknob to get out of the house. I was afraid and so very alone and didn't know what to do about it. I was trapped. All of the things I thought I could do, I couldn't do because my physical self would not accept the commands my brain was supposed to be giving it.

Without a doubt, my brain was not my mind!

My mind was alive and I thought I'd ask God to help me out of this dilemma, although I was angry at him since early childhood. I reasoned if God were really the omnipotent and omniscient being the Christian church had taught me, then he wouldn't have allowed me to suffer. I'd had a hard life as I saw it.

But the God the church taught me about and the God I knew in my heart were very different. The God that the churches taught about was a vengeful God who rules through fear. However, I had wondered why a Creator would discard some of his own creations? That didn't make sense; sounds like an overreaction that we'd ascribe to someone suffering from a serious mental illness today—not a "supreme being."

Upon reflection, I realized that God would accept me regardless of what I had ever done and without expectation of a return-on-investment, and I knew this deep down. Actually I sensed that God was the only true friend I had whom I could trust to help me now.

Indeed I knew that if there was ever a time I needed God, it was now because I was ... dead!

Thus I prayed: "Dear God, my friend, I really need some help here and I know if anyone can help me, it will be you. Will you please help me?"

Then I worried.

I might have seriously messed up this time and, perhaps, it would take more than a "helping hand" to save me? I might need some major repair work to pull my whole self back together again. But soon my prayer was answered, but in a totally unexpected way.

Chapter 4

Rescued by a Being of Light

*"We are like children, who stand in need of masters
to enlighten us and direct us, and God has provided for this,
by appointing his angels to be our teachers and guides."*
—Saint Thomas Aquinas

I glanced toward the outside door.

There I saw an extremely beautiful, spirit being floating exactly the same way I was floating. I knew this being was the answer to my prayer.

He was so awesome!

His feet didn't touch the ground; they just blended into thin air like my own feet did. Yet he had a sort of robe on that was colored a slightly off-white shade. His hair was a light brown, very curly and on the long side of neatness. It shimmered around him as he floated.

His face was pleasant to my eyes. I saw him as an angel without the wings. He looked young, human yet both male and female at the same time. He didn't keep any one form for too long, however, as he shifted shape.

That is to say, if I perceived him to be male, he appeared more male in appearance. If I perceived him to be female, he appeared to be more female. From either point of view there was no real way for me to decide the being's sex for sure. At this point, gender was not all that important to me anyway.

He was all that I had at the moment.

"*The Doors*" song playing in the background now began to fade away.

Then I began to observe that this being was about my height. There was a shimmering glow about him too that was green close to his light body, then blue, then pure white in the outer regions. Speaking metaphorically, he was as beautiful as a butterfly!

He introduced himself; but it was in a language that I didn't understand. So I will refer to him as my guardian angel, or spirit guide, and name him "Bob" for simplicity sake.

Now when Bob spoke to me initially, he said: "I am here to help you." But his mouth didn't move at all. Nor did I actually hear him speak with my ears either. I simply *felt* what he was saying deep within me and there was no doubt whatsoever that he was talking directly to me.

More so, when Bob "spoke" to me, I was no longer afraid. My fears had faded away just like the loud music. A pleasant feeling of warmth and security washed over me, and I felt peace and comfort like I'd never felt before in my life. I thought for a moment that this entity in front of me was God. Bob knew what I was thinking, smiled affectionately and said, "No, I am not God."

Whatever the case, this was the peace I was searching for through my use of alcohol and drugs. It even started to become strangely familiar to me, like I had felt it before but not in this current life. Bob called me by a specific name, too, and I really wish I could remember it. I told him he must have the wrong guy and the name he used for me was not my name.

He chuckled softly and said: "You are a great master. You have merely forgotten who you are."

I didn't want to believe him because I had my own ideas of what a "master" was then and if I were this "great master" I certainly wouldn't have had all of the difficulties I had in my life.

To me, a master was a rich person who kept servants to serve him and maintained control of them, usually through intimidation and fear. I didn't see myself as being served by anyone, rather I felt like I was a servant to everyone else. I felt I was an evil being too, because this is what I had been told in my life several times by those I had been serving and at this point in my life I really did believe I was evil.

It wasn't until later in my experience that I was shown what a master really is and even then it took me an extremely long time to understand what I was shown in that regard.

Bob offered to prove he knew everything about me. He reviewed the things I did when I was a child and what I had only thought about and never, ever expressed to anyone. Basically, he told me my deepest, darkest secrets. He provided some accurate examples of what would cause me to become so depressed and angry so early in my life. He revealed what I thought and felt at bedtime when I was a toddler.

By that time, I had no doubt he knew me, better than I knew myself. Bob communicated that I was someone from history whose name I actually did recognize then. He told me I returned to physical form this time to complete something I started back then.

Bob said, "David" is the name of my body in this particular physical existence. He explained there is much more than I am consciously aware of now: that there is a spirit part of me that has its own name and history.

Bob said I would eventually learn to use the qualities of the physical and spiritual aspects of my "spirit soul self" in this lifetime should I choose to learn about and develop them. He said it was entirely my choice to do this, and if I chose not to apply myself in this way it would be fine, but I would experience the consequences connected to either choice.

Bob told me I was one of the first of my kind on the planet.

That is, I would help populate the planet with special souls whose specific mission is to help their fellow humans restore the planet's harmony within this universe.

Of course, I didn't fully understand it then, but I strongly agreed this planet needs something or someone to help it along. I was highly-skeptical this person could be me.

The expression on Bob's face was pleasant all the time and when he spoke to me he did so in a manner that was positive, assertive and nurturing in tone. He didn't criticize my family or me at all for anything I had done.

In fact, he said nothing that I could possibly construe as negative in tone toward any topic. His language was very eloquent, but I understood most of the main points he made at least.

Then Bob told me I could travel with him to wherever I wanted to go on our planet and in our solar system. He said I could come back and see my body at any time I wanted, although I admit that I was skeptical of that claim. Bob sensed my concern about separating and said my body would be fine without "me" in it—unless I made a personal choice to disconnect my soul from it.

I knew I wanted to leave the house and my childhood neighborhood for certain, but I had difficulty deciding where to go initially. While I trusted Bob, I still had doubts about what he was telling me. I could go ANY-

WHERE? This was a lot for a kid like me to swallow!

Eventually, I decided that I would give him the benefit of my doubt as I didn't sense anything negative from him and had little reason to believe he was some sort of devil.

Yet that was a concern, so I asked Bob about evil. Bob said there are indeed negative entities, probably as many negative ones as there are positive ones in the universe. That does make sense then that life here is a battle between light and dark forces. I recalled the words of Apostle Paul where he said our world is in a sort of tug-of-war between the "powers and principalities of darkness."

Nonetheless, Bob clearly was a positive light being.

And after all, he did come to me as a result of my humbly asking the God of my heart to help me out of a jam. I also felt it was not a good idea to question the answer I was given too much. That is highly-disrespectful to an obviously well-intentioned angel. We are cautioned to "test the spirits" yet that does not mean that we have the right to assign them tasks for "extra credit!"

I'd seen enough proof of his divine powers.

So with a little courage built-up, I felt it would be fun to see the "Seven Wonders of the World." The idea just popped into my mind for some reason. I might have chosen something more profound to see given the wide-range of options I was given, but the Seven Wonders were my first thought. And in retrospect, I did choose as wisely as I could have at the time.

As I contemplated, Bob let out a soft chuckle, then patiently explained that all that was physically left of the Seven Wonders were the pyramids in Egypt and the Grand Canyon in the United States. He said I had already seen that sacred site in the U.S.A. as a boy but if I wanted to go see it again, we could do so - it was not a problem.

The truth was that I simply couldn't think of anywhere else to go, so I told him I would like to see the pyramids in Egypt as well as the rest of the Southwestern United States. He told me to trust him, imagine where I wanted to go, and we'd be there: thus, I focused on the pyramids, and we arrived in Egypt instantly!

Chapter 5

Astral Travel

*"How can you prove whether at this moment we are sleeping,
and all our thoughts are a dream; or whether we are awake,
and talking to one another in the waking state?"*
—Plato

At first, I saw the pyramids as they were in 1979 but also how they were in all of the ancient times, too. I saw them from both points of view. Likewise, and this was miraculous; I saw spirit people without physical bodies from both eras coexisting there in that space, together, both at the same time.

Do we leave parts of our soul energy behind? Is that why the shamans have trance rituals that seek to retrieve one's fragmented selves? It was as if everything in our history was still going on, overlapped and interpenetrated.

Was this the meaning of the idea that if we do not learn from history, we are doomed to repeat it forever? Later I was told that physics calls this concept a "hologram": a word in the Greek language that means "a whole message."

I asked Bob: How could it be that the past and present could be linked together in time, within a single space? He replied that what I was seeing were the energies of these other dimensions in one big dance of light and how they interacted to co-create reality. I saw spirits make choices in the "past" and how their decisions define options for the "future" choices of the spirits in the "present."

Suddenly, I understood that I was a part of this same past that I was observing and felt my existence as a human in this current life related directly to something I did then. From what I could see, I hurt other people through my actions. Therefore, my current life's mission was related to the decisions I made back in Egypt ages ago.

The past and present eras rivaled each other in beauty and from the point of view that I had then, the order, the justice shown in the choices I observed made perfect sense to me as well. While we were there, I was told some things about the pyramids and Egypt that I don't fully remember now. I don't remember the specifics, but the overall intentions pertained to the energies of the planet and the role the pyramids have played and still can potentially play in its restoration.

Facts were given about the function of the pyramids and an explanation of why as well as how they were built. I really do wish I could remember the detailed specifics of what Bob explained while we were there. At a minimum, I know that they were highly significant and had to do with mankind's future survival.

More than likely, I don't remember because I am not ready to remember them yet, or humanity is not ready to receive them yet—or both situations are true. Whatever, my angelic friend did show and explain some of the "why" and "how" of things there. And after Bob brought these to the attention of my "soul" again, I intuitively sensed that it was time to move on.

Besides, now I knew there was so much more that I could see and feel and thereby learn that I didn't want to waste this opportunity on one topic alone.

We left Egypt and proceeded toward the Southwest United States. It was amazing to be able to fly there slowly and see the sights along the way. I saw the entire planet from a low orbit point-of-view, like the astronauts on the Space Shuttle. More so, I could focus on any place on the earth whatsoever, and tell in a glance how healthy it was, or not, by how it felt to me.

Everything has a unique energy frequency vibration!

On the way back to the USA from Egypt, I specifically saw the countries of the Far East and islands in the Pacific Ocean. As we flew I could feel the energies of these places and was told that the oceans are where the energies of the planet are the most natural in nature.

In fact, the oceans contain the energies of the Sun and the Milky Way Galaxy. This is where our planet receives and transmits the infinite loop of information that is exchanged between entities within the cosmos itself.

These energies I saw were aglow, shining, sparkling, about as intense as a pastel, misty rainbow. In particular, I noticed the areas near large cities had a diminished natural energy charge compared to the "undeveloped" or wilder wilderness areas. There were even a few select places on the land that had strong energy signatures rivaling those in the oceans where energies enter and leave the planet—but not many of them.

In general, the consumer lifestyle choices made by human beings had a direct impact on the life force energies in that specific region as well as on the entire planet itself. If humans consumed too many of the local resources, the sensed, or "felt," energy was definitely not the same there. It was like a cell or two in a multi-celled battery had gone dead; it could no longer power-up that landscape, a living habitat for creatures.

Beyond that realization, the energies I saw and felt in the cities of eastern countries like Africa, India, Tibet, even parts of the Middle East were gentler; they had a nicer quality than those I later felt in the United States. Bob let me know that there are groups of people in those countries that are a bit more attuned with the energies of the planet and the universe than we are in the United States.

The energies of the United States felt quite different; they were chaotic, childlike, unbalanced, out-of-control. They seemed tainted, unnatural, and foreign to the long term well-being of the Earth. The purity of energies I saw overseas just wasn't here in our country.

Naturally, I was shocked!

For I thought I'd see bright, huge, dynamic energies in our mighty powerful military-industrial nation.

I wondered why this was so?

Bob stated that the difference in the energies were due to the degree the humans in the United States of America have damaged the land by consuming it in an unsustainable manner in too many regions for far too long now. We are a bloated, fat people, in effect "eating ourselves to death" through our mass weapons of manufacturing that consume nature's reserves of energy without replacing them.

Night was falling in the desert Southwest U.S. when we arrived. Once again, I could see the energies emanating from everything, but especially the plant and animal life. The energy was strongest in the land that had the least amount of humans, in keeping with the formula that I had seen thus far. The asphalt cities of the world were depleted of the life force.

Clearly, we need more Nature Reserves!

It was explained to me that human bodies are the basic producers of energy in the cities, in fact, but because of their relatively low vibration (as compared to nature) the levels were lower. Nonetheless, I could see some higher sources of energy in the cities; these were "spirit people" that had higher energy vibration levels; and some of them actually communicated with Bob.

These higher-level spirit beings were on a mission like Bob, working with humans living in the cities and the special energy places of the world. Some of them were just like my friend and others were more like me. The ones like him were very high in vibration; the ones like me were very low in vibration.

Yes, I could see the reason for the difference in vibration too.

The humans like me were still attached to their "sleeping" physical bodies at the same time that they were having a "waking" lucid dream out-of-body experience. That is to say, the intensity of their vibrations were correlated with whether or not they still had a physical body to power-up employing the spiritual "light" body as its living source of solar power.

I also saw "dark souls."

These are earthbound spirits who refuse to go into the "light." The light is a sort of conduit, tunnel, or porthole that souls can go into if they so choose to do so.

But for them to choose that option, they have to acknowledge that there exists a power greater than themselves, and make a conscious decision to surrender to it. More so, this would require that they then not prey on the energies of other entities still in human form to satisfy their own selfish desires—sexual or otherwise.

However, even when the dark souls do "see the light," and understand the implications, they make a conscious decision not to go to it. They would rather seek to influence other wayward out-of-body souls in pursuit of self-centered passions as well as embodied humans who do not understand what the light is yet—Our Higher Self.

In that sense, there really is little difference in the spirit world than in the physical world, where people are constantly persuading others to make bad choices regarding their selfish lifestyles. I was essentially seeing a mirror image of the human race, as I saw it then, feeding off of one another's life force energy for good and evil.

Bob told me that I would always be protected from those that would select this form of darkness for themselves, as long as I chose to focus on the love within me, and not the negativity. I understood I could even escort the dark ones to the light if I were living in this type of unconditional love and kindness towards others myself.

The dark ones that I saw didn't try to affect us. Yet they did give nasty looks when they saw Bob, and I was so glad to be with him. I never knew this realm of energy existed, and would not, at least consciously, until I "died" again. Then Bob explained the operation of the cosmic energies to me. He was a very patient teacher.

Basically, he said, that we are afloat, swimming in waves of light all the time now. That is, we process our Sun's showering photons of energy through our human body, after they've been captured by the magnetic fields and molten core of our Earth. We then condition or shape this field of energy surrounding and flowing within us through expressing the intentions of our hearts to the living beings that we come in contact with animals, plants, and humans. Ideally, our "love" energy will restore our planet to wellness too.

This knowledge and second sight is important in the future as we are able to see the colors of energy in the beings that live in these other realms. Bob said the more brilliant the color is around a being, the higher the vibration of consciousness present within them. He said seeing this "aura" of the soul is very useful in determining how much a particular spirit needs to work on his or her development in fact. Spirit beings of higher vibration know how to help human beings of lower vibration and earthbound souls as well.

All souls have this field of energy: **It is the light of life itself!**

The energy of the aura of a human is what links it to the human body, the planet, the Sun—and beyond. The aura's absence from the body is what we humans understand to be "death." After death, the aura that contains the thoughts and feelings of the being separates and transitions back again into its soul body of light.

Bob said I am of the same energy type as he, but my vibrations are lower when I am in human form. In time my energy would raise to match his intensity provided I chose to take the initiative to consciously evolve my soul in a positive way. He told me that the best way to do that is to show love and live in harmony with the planet, all of its beings, and with my human body.

Bob talked a bit more about the dark souls who would attempt to influence my spiritual growth in a negative way and said I would know them by discerning their intent. If what they said or did detracted from the harmony of the planet in any way, they would be harnessing the negative spectrum of universal energy.

Further, I understood as a being of the light, I am a part of the positive energies of the Source of Life, and I probably should weigh carefully decisions and thoughts that contribute to the negative part of creation. More so, if the intent of an entity is only for their own good, or is detrimental to someone else, it would be an indication of negative vibration and I might want to consider this when I interact with them.

Nonetheless, I was not to judge them. Bob said that if I wished to choose the negative type of intent, I too was free to do so. But by universal law I would certainly have to face the consequences of what I have chosen to manifest into the creation long-term.

Interestingly, negative energy was originally meant to be a tool to enhance the evolution of souls, but over time we abused the tool and the privilege of free-will.

Positive and negative energies properly balanced is the intent of the Creator. This concept worked well with nature until the free-will choices of humanity tipped the scales on the energy equation, when we began slowly moving away from loving one another and the planet as one single being and allowed self-service to rule.

So, what is "sin" really? It is ego!

Bob informed me there is much going on with this planet that spirits can see but which humans cannot see with their physical eyes because their vibrations are so low now that their third eye is clamped-shut. So my wise mentor explained beings of higher vibration do live on Earth, but they are not human, they are part of the living being called Gaia. The term folks in metaphysical circles used is "elementals."

By example, Bob showed me the life in the trees and inside the earth that I could see readily then as a spiritual body, but couldn't see when back in my physical body later.

He explained these beings were the caretakers of physical life on the planet; indeed take care of what we too casually call "nature"—the plant life, the mineral life, and the waterborne life. These ethereal beings work to ensure all aspects of the Earth remain balanced, protected, and healthy so that it stays alive at all costs.

Bob said that Gaia has her own energy source in the space that she is embedded and is really a true living being by all standards, one of the most significant spiritual entities of our own universe.

She is a beautiful lady of abundance in fact!

However, he said if humans choose to abuse Gaia by not observing the harmonic balance of nature, consuming too much too fast, this harms Gaia as it alters her designed energy structure, forcing her to compensate via minor and major Earth Changes.

Truly, it is not nice to fool with Mother Nature!

Bob said humans are the ones who manipulate her energy through their choices. I saw examples of how humans have deforested the planet and reduced the energy available faster than it could be replenished through the process of nature's life cycles.

In particular, I saw the energies of the land in the Pacific Northwest region of the United States. The contrast of the energies between the areas where the trees had been removed from clear-cutting and where they remained in tact or selectively pruned was clearly evident to me.

Bob explained that although Gaia was very strong, she has been weakened considerably since humans have chosen to use resources like trees, oil, and minerals in a manner inconsistent with the replenishment laws of the universe. The key idea is to use the resources no faster than Gaia can reproduce them.

For once the base magnetic energy signature is altered by consuming the planet's living resources in an unsustainable manner Gaia has to alter her vibration to readjust her orbit, thus redistributing her energy patterns. But this disturbance in the field of energy disrupts the harmony of the spheres and thus impacts the planet as well as the rest of the solar system even if ever so slightly.

Recall that it only takes a small disturbance in the flow of energy to create chaos. The example from weather studies now uses the metaphor: When a butterfly flaps its wings in Japan, a tornado touches down in Kansas.

All of this made sense to me because I knew that I was doing the same thing to my own body when I abused substances. Not only was I hurting me, I was hurting everyone else around me as well through my own bad choices. When using mind-body altering chemical substances, I, too, was shifting my magnetic energy signature.

For instance, if I were fearful or angry, the energies I put out into the "empty space" bred more of the same and those sensations were detected by all those within my sphere of influence. Now I wanted to see how our planet looked energetically as well so I asked Bob: Can we go into space and see Gaia's energy patterns from a distance?

Bob said "Yes!"

So I concentrated my thought on my goal, and we then soared into what is known as "empty space." I did not hesitate at all this time for I knew now that I was a light being with the only limits being the ones I place on myself. Flying away from this planet I could see Gaia was breathtakingly beautiful and so very full of life activity! I could see the magnificent glow of living light surrounding her. Indeed the colors of that aura alone affected me greatly at that moment.

Spontaneously, I projected all of my love to her.

I felt very peaceful and blessed to see and feel the planet in her glory. I knew that beyond a doubt, she is a conscious living being and I loved her dearly then. Her aura was the most brilliant blue I have yet to see anywhere. I learned it would have been even more beautiful if it weren't for the destruction humans have dealt their biosphere since we came to Gaia and that saddened me.

The Great Lady moved in space and I could hear and understand that the sound was the energy flowing in and out of her at the north-south poles. It reminded me of the song I heard my body playing when I was lying in the lounge chair in the house, but of course it was infinitely grander in scale. Clearly, nature is singing a song itself.

In other words, the living things we call "nature" are required for a human soul to maintain a physical body, so we can have access to the energies of the universe. Gaia has been created for our spirit to play, learn, and grow physically like a caterpillar preparing to manifest as a butterfly.

Bob then blew my mind: He said that humans were designed to live eternally on Gaia and are not meant to "die!"

He said "dying" means little in the spirit world because everything is alive, just in different forms. The reason humans "die" is because they have fallen away from the balance of nature. That is, we are inevitably impacted, negatively and positively, by the energies we shape by our choices for both bad and good outcomes.

Bob explained that humans have fallen away from living in balance with nature and because of this have shortened the time available for them to be in a physical form. This discussion made me wonder: how did humans come to be on Gaia in the first place?

Bob told me I had been part of the original human family here. So I asked my guardian angel: What was Gaia like in the beginning of time and in a flash of light, I was suddenly on Gaia again but not with the same scenery before me now:

I was in a green, lush tropical-type landscape!

Everything was so perfect and warm and felt so right. I remember waking up, standing, and then walking about to explore my surroundings. However, no sooner had I felt a longing to stay there forever, I was back in deep space in my soul body continuing my previous journey of exploration.

Nonetheless, Bob explained some things about where I went but I do think that I may also have gotten a bit too inquisitive at that point and that memory was erased!

This much I know, I was given either a glimpse of our ancient past, or maybe of what Gaia could be like in the future? Either way, it was very inspiring and packed with intense feelings of joy, and I would not mind feeling that way again sometime real soon!

However, Bob impressed upon me this fact: Humans must remember and consciously understand to seek the harmonic balance in all things if they want to survive as a race and live eternally on Gaia forever. Accordingly, I asked if that meant that we humans would eventually transcend "death" and become "immortal" in the way originally intended for us?

The answer came back a resounding ... Y-e-s!

Bob said it was still possible for humans to restore this harmony and it is the next goal that humanity must attain. How long it would take depends on the choices humans make as individuals, and collectively as a whole species sharing the resources of Gaia.

Indeed, I was told humans would eventually realize they must restore the harmony, yet GREAT DAMAGE will be inflicted before we fully realize what we have done to Gaia and choose to work overtime to reverse what we have done to nature.

The damage inflicted will be to humans as well as to Gaia.

Our individual choices will add to the collective energy and that is what will determine the outcome for us. I understood I could contribute best to the eventual restoration of the harmony of the planet by making sure that my thoughts, words, and deeds are designed by my intent to provide as much as possible, a positive outcome for everyone.

As I watched Gaia's energy signature pulsate, I reflected on what I was feeling, hearing, and seeing—and it made perfect sense to me finally. I could see plainly how my life really does matter. We are each like battery cells of consciousness that is comprised of information that is energy itself. As I contemplated what I was being shown, I asked Bob about the other parts of the solar system that my thoughts affected.

I looked toward the moon, focused on it, and once more, suddenly we were there on the surface. Albeit I saw very little of the glowing energies I saw on Gaia, and asked why the moon was so different? I was told that one of the moon's minor functions is to provide a rest stop for travelers like us.

Yet, more so, the moon's main function is to serve Gaia by helping her remain aligned with the Sun, planets, and rest of the universe. The moon is a filter, or governor, of the energies and that keeps Gaia from being overwhelmed by them. It also serves as a type of two-way conduit that coordinates the transference of energy from Gaia to the rest of the universe. Of course, I began to think of all of the other planets in our solar system too now. Then I wondered about the stars. For if Gaia and the moon were so connected, where would the other planets and stars fit into this design?

Instantly, we traveled toward the other planets, and stars, at a totally immeasurable speed-of-light.

What a rush!

Chapter 6

The Universe

*"You are a child of the Universe, no less than the moon and the stars;
you have a right to be here. And whether or not it is clear to you,
no doubt the Universe is unfolding as it should."*
—Max Ehrmann

As funny as it may sound, I simply looked at all of the stars I could see visually, and then picked the first one that I felt called me by name. It was as if a latent memory was surfacing. We then zoomed past all of the planets in our own solar system on our way to this star that I had chosen—or it had chosen me.

I knew that I chose a star in the Little Dipper.

Interestingly enough, as we slowed down when we neared a planet I could see its aura and hear its energies just like Gaia. Each planet sang a song that sounded differently than the other, but friendly and inviting as well. Truly, there is a living music of the spheres.

I also saw souls on every one of those planets!

I understood each planet is a place for souls to live, learn, and evolve. Bob said each planet has a proper name and a general theme for spiritual growth. He told me these souls practice managing the energy on the other planets to prepare to experience Gaia.

I saw great cities on every one of those planets!

Now I wondered: How could there be cities there and why humans didn't seem to know of them? We are not primitives: I mean we have high-tech telescopes!

Bob was amused.

Albeit he patiently explained that there are many facets of life in the universe not readily seen by humans. Most souls in physical human form have yet to attain the higher vibration required to see multi-dimensional, energy beings from the universe.

Then Bob said Gaia is the ultimate experience for a soul because we evolve faster here than anywhere else as it is so difficult to apply what we learn on those other planets. These lessons require a physical form that can experience aging, pain, suffering, death, and Gaia provides means for a soul to do that in blunt terms.

Bob said souls pick a physical life on Gaia. No one is forced to come here against their will. I understood that I had picked the parents I was born to, so they could help me learn what I needed in order to grow my soul and to help other souls grow too. Equally, I was being told and shown these things, so I could help souls return Gaia to harmony by coming together at a later point in my life.

We soon arrived at what I like to call "my" star.

The star looked like it was sucking the energies of space into itself. If I had to describe this scene, I would compare it to a whirlpool, a tornado, or perhaps a tunnel or even a drain of some sort. It spun like a hurricane, and had a distinct center eye to it that was very calm.

This was intriguing; I could see, hear, and feel there was something on the other side of that vortex. I wanted to go there badly as if a magnet was pulling me, but I can't really explain that sensation in words or even what I knew then.

Bob said if I applied myself to the tasks I was given and grew my soul enough on Gaia, eventually I would be able to go to the other side of the star and handle what I find there. Yet he strongly suggested that I not go further into this experience until I was really ready to do so. I understood Bob loved me deeply and felt him to be much wiser than I, so I respected his suggestion and let this opportunity pass from me.

I asked Bob about God instead.

Again, I cannot remember the specifics of what he showed me. Most of that information, however, had to do with the size and physical structure of this universe and God's role in it. I do recall that God is the base essence of all there is in existence. That this essence extends beyond the creation I was seeing, for God seeks the assistance and companionship of other beings like himself.

Bob said it is likely impossible that I could understand what "God" is all about, but I was assured that God loves us, the Lady Gaia, and this universe deeply, much as devoted human parents love their spouse and children on Gaia. That idea of unconditional love brought me to the thought of Jesus and I immediately wanted to know more about him.

So I asked: Who is Jesus, really?

Bob told me Jesus is one of the great masters who made an agreement with God to come here and be an example for humans on how to act toward each other so that they find their way back to the path of harmony with Gaia. I was told Jesus is but one of many such masters entrusted by God to help souls evolve here and elsewhere. Bob said Jesus is higher in vibration than many other masters.

He said that God holds the master Jesus in high favor because he is perhaps the most widely known example on Gaia of what humans can attain because he attained his mastery the very same way we can, if we choose to work toward it!

I then got to see the master I felt to be Jesus.

He joined us and, at first, looked similar to how the church taught me he looked from the classic paintings. However, I did not see him like that for very long because he changed into his light alone. Jesus' light was the purest display of energy I have ever seen. There was no need for words to be exchanged between us as powerful loving and kind feelings swept over me like a tidal wave of emotion that I cannot even begin to describe. The best was yet to come:

This great master spirit took me within **himself.**

Then Jesus shared that loving one another unconditionally is what souls must do in order for peace and harmony to become fully-felt on Gaia. He said only that, nothing more, and then he slowly faded away into space. This experience of a lifetime came and went like a candle in the wind. But those few words were all that I needed to hear, and I knew it as I understand this much: The cosmos is full of servants to God!

Later Bob told me that a clearly established hierarchy of light beings, angels, are in fact dedicated to preserving the harmony of the universe. They carefully help plan the inner workings of all there is in creation. I understood humans are perhaps the most important part of the harmonic balance because they have free will. That is, humans can provide great service to God, too, provided they accept the responsibility of serving each other unselfishly.

After Bob explained a few more things in that regards, I was shown our whole solar system all at once in full-color and sound. The planets were in a straight line configuration now. I could see the entire row of them from Pluto to the Sun as well as hear and feel the symphony they played; it was awesome.

I felt so very blessed by this gift of wisdom and extremely important, yet I still didn't understand why I deserved such an incredible experience as this one. There I was, a spirit who usually went out of my way to inflict pain on other souls, but regardless of who I thought I was on Gaia, I was deeply-loved, and needed for the larger plan of God to manifest.

In fact, I was given answers to questions that I am sure many people wonder about all of their lives. Likewise I was happy to know that the answer to all the problems we have on this planet is nor more complex than to love one another as God loves us. It seems that this is the way the energy can flow most easily through us when we are in balance, harmonically-tuned and resonant with nature.

I thanked Bob for these precious insights but he expressed that there was much more for him to show me, if I was ready to experience it. I told him I was ready. I still didn't know why I was chosen for this blessing beyond description, but I wasn't about to question why at this stage either. I had to go with the flow! Any doubts that I had harbored about this whole experience heretofore, vanished. I gave myself over to him completely.

We retreated from the star in front of us.

Chapter 7

The "Hidden" Spirit City

"You live on Earth for only a few short years
which you call an incarnation,
and then you leave your body as an outworn dress
and go for refreshment to your true home in spirit."
—White Eagle

We headed back to the Lady Gaia.

Then I saw it: A great Spirit City that was located just above what we would call the atmosphere of our planet. These were beautiful white-colored buildings as far as I could see in every direction; they were made of wooden frames with plants merging into them. I saw spirits living there all having a unique vibration, but no real physical body presence like I was accustomed to on the surface of Gaia.

The inhabitants of the city went in and out of these buildings, going to work and play. They were as diverse as we humans are on the surface of our globe. I saw a fountain-like well where spirits went to get what I think to be the equivalent of water—spirit energy? There were no vehicles there at all. Spirits there got around the same way Bob and I got around, they floated and flew. It was a pretty busy place. There were many souls there in that magical space above the clouds.

This Spirit City had no boundaries that I could see, a place full of life of every kind, too. There were plants, trees, and water just like on Gaia, but they were more pure in essence.

Nature was absolutely perfect there!

It was untainted by human manipulation and decisions to harm one another were non-existent. The place was very similar to Gaia; all that was missing were the problems and negativity. This place had an extremely positive vibration and was, what I believe is called heaven in earth terms.

I saw souls going between Spirit City and Gaia with and without guardian angels.

Interestingly, I could determine their level of development in fact by feeling the energy they emanated. I could see and feel animal souls were also going back and forth like humans were doing, seeking replenishment. Some were sad, beaten, and scared, much like I felt before Bob appeared to me in the party house.

The beings that were returning to this wonderful home full of love, light, and positive energy were ready to enjoy their time without physical bodies.

This was like a rest stop on the highway to the stars!

Bob took me inside one of the larger buildings where I saw spirits doing jobs similar to those on Gaia. I saw people working artistically with simple paint and paper to tasks that I could not recognize.

There were also classrooms where souls were learning all about earth, its purpose and operation. The spirits were engaged in what we would consider the arts here more than anything else. What was going on in this place was however firmly connected to Gaia's long-term wellbeing.

When we moved past the spirits that were working, they looked at me because I was with Bob. We glided up some stairs where I met a few select spirit persons who knew me and I recognized them from somewhere too. There was one who seemed sad, another who was painting something, and two more happily playing together. They all greeted me warmly and asked how I was doing on Gaia?

They honestly knew and were happy to see me again. Each of them gave me advice of which I have no conscious memory.

Initially, I thought I was going to be given a job there, but Bob felt my thought and told me there was something I needed to do first.

I was ecstatic!

I was in "heaven" despite everything I'd done and experiencing what most people on Gaia probably only dream about and hope for as an afterlife. The love I felt there was the same love I felt when I was with the light of Master Jesus no doubt about it.

Clearly, this is the place of belonging that I was searching for on Gaia during my restless moments. I wanted the feeling of meaning and safety that I sensed here to last forever. I was truly happy; I was really home, and I knew it immediately.

I was ready to stay in Spirit City and perform whatever function I was assigned to do without question now.

Bob then took me to another building more special than the rest. It was much bigger and had the greenest foliage I have ever seen growing on it, decorating it like a shrine. Many spirits came into and left from this place and I could tell it was very, very special to them.

This building was alive; we entered reverently.

The entire inside of the building was decorated with this glowing wood paneling that Bob said was from trees that grow in this wonderful city. He asked me to wait on a bench made of this "living wood" while he went through the double doors on my right.

As I sat there, I began to feel strangely familiar with my surroundings. In fact, it was as if I had been here many times before. It was a really strong déjà vu all over again. I was curious, of course, but not enough to put all the pieces of the puzzle together yet.

This much I knew: I had been on this bench before and for the same purpose—self-evaluation. I realized I wasn't here to play games, nor was I here for a friendly visit. I began to see visions of my past lives unfolding, a big living tapestry wanted to come forth into my conscious awareness.

Suddenly, Bob came out of the room.

It was time for me to go in there now. He said he would wait until I came out and told me not to worry. He cautioned that I was to be truthful with the beings in the room in the event they asked me tricky questions. He said their job was not to judge.

Rather, they were the ones who collect and present a soul's records to them. They had access to all of one's life events. Bob told me to remember who I was as a spiritual being and to refrain from fear, and he would patiently wait for me.

Honestly, I was scared to leave him, but I knew in my heart that I would always be protected by my guardian angel, so I gathered myself together. I reached out and turned one of the golden knobs and then walked gingerly through those glowing double-wide wooden living doors. Yes, I could grasp objects here again I noted.

Chapter 8

Everything Returns

"Know one knows whether death,
which people fear to be the greatest evil,
may not be the greatest good."
—Plato

Once inside, I saw a group of spirits gathered at a round table that was made of the same glowing wood that was perfect in every way imaginable. These spirit beings had the highest vibration I had felt so far with the exception of Master Jesus.

I looked at these serious-minded beings and immediately began to recognize them as I felt their energy sweep over me. They were all definitely familiar even though I knew not why that was the case yet.

Indeed they looked at me and I knew beyond a doubt that I had been in this very room before where sacred business matters were conducted. Equally, I understood that each being in the group had their own specialty to represent in terms of the human personality. They each had an aspect of me within them that they were responsible to know about to the minutest detail.

I felt a deep sense of respect for them, but feared them because of their obvious high status in the scheme of life and death and rebirth. I feared a couple of them more than others as I *felt* their power ripple through my own being.

All of a sudden, I saw my parents on Gaia; this was before I was born. I saw how their coming together as a married couple came about and watched my brother and sister be born before me. I saw my parent's positive and negative sides and selected them according to the obstacles that I had planned to be confronting on Gaia myself. The group then wanted to know from my perspective why I picked these particular parents.

They said that I knew how and why and asked me to tell them now.

Specifically, I chose my parents so that I could assist them on their paths as well as to achieve my learning objectives, too. I agreed on this mutually-beneficial relationship before we even came to Gaia to live out this lifetime's scenarios.

The visions became clearer as I recollected on my purpose, and I saw my soul go inside of my mother's womb.

I was fascinated to see that I traveled from Spirit City on nothing more than a **Ray of Sunlight,** safely encapsulated within a tunnel, until securely locked into my mother's body. Once I was in the womb, there was no way to return to the spirit world, and I was fully aware of it. I felt very constricted in there, trapped, claustrophobic really, as I didn't have the freedom to travel anywhere.

Ironically, as it came time to be born into this realm I was afraid to come out of the womb. I did not want to lose the degree of protection it afforded me from the fury of the outside world.

But I saw myself being born and it was from both an observer viewpoint as well as reliving the actual experience. I remember going down the birth canal and into the bright light of this life. I felt the doctor's cold hands and the warm smiles of the nurses. Overall, however, I experienced the harshness of being born again.

I saw myself as a helpless infant who needed his mother for everything. I experienced the extremes of my mother's and father's emotions; their love as well as their anger.

Equally, I saw all of the good and all of the bad events from my childhood years. I experienced the choices I made and the impact they had on my life. I was able to see and feel everything significant that happened from every angle, including the perspective of the other humans that my choices affected. I felt the full range of my emotions as well as the emotions of the souls I had hurt as well as loved.

I must admit: what I saw was surprising because there were more sides to these events than I allowed myself to be aware of on any given day. As I watched I thought, "I never knew that," or "I wish I'd known that!" For instance, I saw why my father left me as a child, and why I experienced the neglect and abuses I endured afterward. Seeing and feeling the big picture allowed me to better understand the cause and effect to my life's circumstances. All in all, I learned that it matters deeply what choices you and I make while we are on Gaia as it shapes the world around us from that point onwards.

In my particular case, I saw my father leaving us when I was three years old, and I realized his decision pained him too. I understood why he left and why I became so sad and angry about it. Indeed I learned just how powerful we humans are and how we can affect each other in positive and negative ways, whether we're aware of it or not. It was amazing to see how my innocent choices had such a powerful effect on souls I had no idea I was impacting.

That traumatic realization is one I will never forget ever.

I experienced the whole spectrum of *feelings* of my life in a relatively short period of "time," as we humans sense it. I saw these things without the filters I usually activate when I am in physical form. You see, where I was, time did not really exist and the veil my ego places on my thought processes didn't seem to exist there either. Everything I did in my life affected the evolution of the souls connected to me as that charged-energy radiated throughout them and creation itself.

I saw the reasons for all my actions, so there was a logical place for all of my positive and negative intentions. That is, there was no action that was necessarily wrong, but there were actions I took that didn't enhance positive growth in me or in others.

When I made choices that were purely for my own benefit—selfish—the resulting feelings of others were less than positive, be that anger, fear, sadness or other negative reactions. I was both a victim and a beneficiary of the actions I was shown.

If the result of my actions from a global perspective were on the negative side of the scale, I was able to see the reasons for it and how I could have acted differently. From this panoramic viewpoint I learned what was and was not working to bring about a positive effect.

Here was the bottom line: If I made choices that provided benefit to others without the expectation of a return from them, the resulting feelings I felt were positive, loving, kind, and enjoyable. If the results of my choices were not of service to others, I would get to feel their pain as well as know that if I made similar choices I would create more of the same feeling again and again and again.

Needless to say, this wasn't really an enjoyable experience for me to go through. I saw that many of my choices fostered negative effects, but I also learned how enjoyable the review would have been had I chosen to affect other souls positively most of the time.

Chapter 9

Options to Consider

"We must be the change we wish to see."
—Mahatma Gandhi

After my life records were presented to the group, and reviewed by all of us, they asked me some questions about what I saw and how I felt about my life up to then. I knew I had to provide an honest assessment and I could not lie to them period.

Then I turned right around and hesitated a bit when they asked me whether I affected others more positively than negatively.

You bet I thought about lying and saying I affected others more positively, but I concluded that would not be the wisest thing for me to do at this point in the process. Though I had this idea that if I said "more positive" I would actually have more of a chance at staying here in Spirit City and that was what I wanted more than anything else.

Nonetheless, the group knew what I was thinking, so I had to tell them the truth: I could have done a better job on Gaia. Likewise I recalled that what I had come to earth to accomplish was well underway but I knew I wasn't finished yet.

They agreed and told me I still had many things to do and that I might want to go back and do them now. I was told it was understood how difficult it would be for me, but it was necessary to finish my path as I had originally planned it.

Evidently I set lofty goals for my life and the earthly events I was experiencing were aimed towards those outcomes. The group said I came to Gaia to both learn and share with others using the wisdom that I have accumulated over several lifetimes. They explained that I am needed here to help souls bring themselves and Gaia back into perfect balance and harmony with all life forms in nature.

Moreover, I understood what I had experienced thus far were but "baby-steps" preparing me to make a larger contribution to the universe. Their task I saw was NOT to judge me after all. Judging my actions was my job totally through "feeling" the impact I had on the entire creation and they provided the wisdom to do so in a helpful and safe manner.

Upon conclusion, I told the group I was tired and wanted to stay because life on Gaia is hard and unforgiving. I even told them I felt my return would be dangerous because I was not advanced enough in my spiritual evolution. The group said this was precisely why it would be in my best interest to go back to Gaia. They offered that I was more advanced than I was willing to accept though not using the wonderful tools that I carry within my heart.

Although they did say it was possible for me to stay in Spirit City.

But I would need to finish my work on Gaia sooner or later, thereby any delay would only prolong the completion of what I promised to do. They explained the most efficient and least complicating way to do this chore would be to go back to Gaia as soon as possible.

I was stunned and a bit angry as well.

It was like I was given a gift of freedom by knowing but that was then promptly going to be taken away. I resorted to bargaining with the group but it was no use.

These beings understood me, and they remained firm. They would not bargain, most likely because they were basing their advice on facts from my life review that added-up the same way every time. They were experts in these matters of self-evaluation and had all the data as to how to best deal with adversity. So it was up to me; I had a decision to make that was really the hardest decision I would ever make, at least in this lifetime, and I knew it. It was time to go.

I left the room with a great reluctance.

I was very sad indeed that I could not remain in this great place of love, learning, and compassion. Here I thought I was all done on Gaia and was going to move on to a higher plane of existence, but I was not ready to do so and I could feel it.

Honestly, I was fearful of going back to Gaia because of the wisdom I had just gleaned from this life review experience. Knowing the way life and death really worked in terms of positive and negative thoughts and feelings would make things more difficult for me, as I knew full well that Gaia could be a dangerous place for a soul.

It is easy to backslide and not love God and each other as ourself for temptations abound that lead us to do otherwise. We are confronted again and again with circumstances, people that don't fit our mold for perfection, and thus we judge them unworthy of our blessings.

Free will is a gift we have for sure, but our choices are influenced by many hidden variables that we have no control over at a given moment. And thereby we make mistakes based upon our ignorance that have long-term consequences. For instance, if feelings from the heart are not followed they can cause a major negative effect much more than anyone can possibly comprehend.

Our heart is a supercomputer that calculates the impact of thoughts and feelings upon others and ourselves with respect to integrity. Are we saying and doing things that add or subtract from the peacefulness and well-being of mankind? Our cardiovascular pump is the ultimate truth meter! Thus I respected the dangers of staying here with my mission unfulfilled as well as returning to Gaia and the demands that requires; but the decision was mine to make now.

I met Bob outside the conference room.

I told him what happened and asked Bob if I could just stay with him. I had learned a great deal from my guardian angel and I wanted to learn more, all that he could teach me. Bob agreed, but said I needed patience, that I ought to weigh the decision in my heart very carefully before I finally decided on a course of action.

I asked Bob if there was a way I could see ahead and use what I saw to assist in my decision? He said it was permissible up to a point, so Bob showed me in my mind's eye what would happen to me if I chose to return to Gaia. These were future things that would happen in my own personal lifetime.

In particular, Bob showed me that my life would have hardships that would continue for about 20 more years from that time. He said I would have problems finding and maintaining employment, thus lack of money would be a chronic condition as well. He also said I would have this experience with me always, however, I would face obstacles that would keep me from sharing what I have learned in the immediate future.

Bob said people would eventually seek me out to help them answer their own questions about life-after-death and the world of spirit. He said I would be a healer of souls and I would assist other healers in the completion of their duties.

I also learned that I would marry and have several children.

Bob explained that children are extremely important to Gaia's future and part of my task is to nurture and protect mine so their tasks could be completed properly. Even though I had this knowledge, my marriage wouldn't be a very happy one until I mastered how to handle my energies in a positive way.

Bob said that once I had learned to accentuate the positive side of life most of the time, I would be evolved enough to share my learning with other souls. Seemingly, I had the potential to be a big help to folks who wanted to raise their energy to this level of service to the planet now.

In order to do this I was told it would be best to refrain from drugs and alcohol so that I might exert more of my focus on serving others, and have the health to carry my mission to completion, rather than hiding from the world in a self-medicated mental fog. These substances would lower my vibration greatly and thus hinder my performance.

In pragmatic terms, Bob said that I'd be prone to punishment from the authorities on Gaia if I were to continue to use illegal drugs. He said it was likely I would lose my physical freedoms and be thrown into jail sooner or later.

Bob also explained that these mood-altering substances distort the feeling of confidence I needed to perform my tasks. Only until I deemed myself worthy enough of such first-class treatment by making my mind-body pure and strong enough to contain these higher energies, would I be able to complete my tasks that I'd selected. To drive the point home, Bob told me a friend of mine would die in an accident soon.

He would be "drunk," as we call it, driving a car when this happened and I would contribute to it happening. Again, it was my lifestyle that would impact another. Yet I would eventually learn how, when, and with whom to share this wisdom I was given. But in the end, it was still really the person who chooses to be influenced in negative ways because it is their choice as to how to navigate life's highways and byways.

As those insights began sinking in, I asked Bob if I decided to return when would I be finished on Gaia? He said I would return to my current spiritual state of being only after I'd touched enough souls in a positive manner, and could answer the group's questions, spontaneously and without any hesitation, as to my worthiness to be there.

Eventually, Bob said, I'd develop skills that affect others in a positive way in this life, if I made choices that came from my heart not just my head. That after I was finished with this task, I could move on to complete an even higher purpose in a form just like his, a body of light. Then trips back and forth to Gaia would be optional for me as well.

Then my great friend took me to a garden space where I could sit to think over my choices and make my decision. I had to stay here or go to Gaia, again.

Chapter 10

The Decision

"The universal law of karma is that of action and reaction,
cause and effect, sowing and reaping.
In the course of natural righteousness man,
by his thoughts and actions, becomes the arbiter of his destiny."
—Yogananda

I glided into this beautiful garden to make my decision.

It was very peaceful and serene there and I was alone. I sat on a white stone bench to assess my options.

I reflected upon how amazing it was that I still had the free will to make the "wrong" decision, at least one that could go against my true feelings and could produce a negative result. Even in the afterlife choices still had to be made and like all choices they impacted creation.

In this setting, I found myself thinking of my choices and the role I played in the life process as well as the great gift of knowledge I was just given moments ago.

Reflecting upon these lessons-learned, I contemplated what remaining in Spirit City would cost long-term. I thought of the family I was to create and what the effect would be to them and the other souls on Gaia should I choose not to return and share my insights into the hereafter.

Equally, I thought of how wonderful Gaia is and how I saw firsthand what humans do to Gaia when they do not focus on being loving and kind to every life form living here now. I considered the effects on the universe, however small, if I chose to stay in this wonderful place of rest and take the longer way toward my goals, simply be patient and wait on another lifetime to get it right.

Then it dawned on me that much of my thinking to stay in Spirit City was based on selfishness. Staying here would serve me mostly, no one else. The truth of the matter, I was still looking for an excuse not return to Gaia. Since the effect of me choosing to stay would benefit me mostly, I realized that I wouldn't be making the choice out of love for the universe, or for the souls in it, by staying on vacation!

Bob called me a master I recalled, but what I remembered the most was the Master Jesus and the simple wisdom he shared with me. He did not say for me to get as much I could by forgetting or manipulating the feelings of other people – rather that humans need to love one another. I thought about the service-oriented tone of my review also.

More than anything else, I'd need to be of positive service to others if I were to truly become a master, and to help others on their journey in a manner that promotes harmony with all existence. As I mulled over what I wanted to do, I suddenly realized what "mastery" really is in fact.

Mastery is the level of self-sacrifice attained through many lifetimes of pain and suffering, growing one's soul wisdom towards compassion for life itself. A true master who shares their experience of life with other souls, is, therefore in service to them. Masters help provide guidance by example, showing others what they might need to learn in order to attain mastery for themselves. Indeed, this insight finally made sense of what we mean today by the concept of "spirituality" versus religion:

In a nutshell, religion is rules, spirituality is service!

No doubt religion can be seen, in many cases, as counterproductive to the plan of salvation as we cannot serve two masters, fear and love are polar opposites! Thus, a master can be anyone who lives to serve, and serves to live, not someone whose main focus is to rule over others and make them do his bidding for his or her own personal gain. Examining everything from that perspective helped me make my decision: I decided to return to Gaia.

A few decades on Gaia isn't all that long compared to forever, is it? Based on the blessings that I received, I needed to make a service-oriented decision, one that ought to focus on the needs of the other souls connected to me. So, I was ready; I called for my sweet, special angel guide Bob. He appeared to me immediately and I told him of my decision to return.

Bob was brimming with joy!

He told me he would help me when I needed help on Gaia for his advancement depended in part on how successful he was at influencing me in the evolution of my soul.

Bob told me I had helped him very much through my decision and he had always loved me but loved me even more now! He told me he looked forward to the future that I originally chose and was choosing yet again.

My guardian angel was very excited, and I was now too! Although I loved Spirit City, I felt an urgency to return to Gaia as soon as possible so I'd get back here faster with more memories I mused.

Bob then explained to me the procedure for souls returning to Earth is to drink water from the great river of life flowing through the heart of Spirit City. This holy water's purpose is to protect souls going back from knowing too much from their experiences of the afterlife. Somehow the water provided a "forgetting." The idea behind it is for souls to experience Gaia in a natural way, evolve without experiencing "separation anxiety," as a psychologist would call it.

Anyway, Bob said I did not have to drink the water before I went to Gaia, but he touched my "lips" to help me forget the bigger things I cannot share. The things I "forgot" were ideas that if shared with the wrong people would cause problems for them. I was to remember only items useful to me to complete my mission while being most effective in my service to others.

Then Bob said that when I was ready I could go back to Gaia but that he would be in close contact to help guide and protect me while it remained part of his purpose to do so, and as I needed it. This helped me to relax and feel much better about returning to the planet while knowing that I would eventually return to Spirit City. This knowledge still provides me with great peace today: I also knew I was a great asset to the energies of humans, Gaia, and the universe.

What a comfort to know death does not exist!

The moment arrived to go and I began my return trip to Gaia by following the trail of light energy that was still part of and connected to my physical body on Earth.

As I descended from these higher realms of our sky, I remember first seeing the water tower at the Detroit Zoo. This tower was a landmark, silver in color and easily recognizable; I saw that the energies of the zoo were the most intense in this region as well.

In particular, I was enjoying seeing the auras on everything light-up as the sun began to rise. I gave serious thought to roaming about, checking out more places on the planet before returning to my physical body, but decided against it because I knew it could be dangerous. I didn't want to be negatively-impacted by the dark souls' energy that I saw were in these lower realms as well.

I felt my purpose was too important to chance being lured away from the positive path I was returning to tread on now. I knew I needed to be careful and that it might be best to move on quickly and just do what I needed to do instead of fooling around and getting myself into trouble.

So that's what I did; I went straight to my home and observed my sleeping family. Out of curiosity, more than anything else, I wanted to see them before I got back into my body. I saw their auras and knew they needed compassion and love—not my criticism and judgment.

I willingly projected some of my caring energy towards them as that is what my family really needed from me. I knew now that I could give this energy freely out of true love for them. And that they too are on the paths they need to be on, but together I can learn much from them and they can learn much from me. I'd been putting big conditions on my love for them and I saw that this was wrong.

If I learned only one thing from Spirit City, it was that true love is unconditional and placing any conditions on it takes the "true" part away. Indeed if it weren't for unconditional love, I certainly would not have had the overwhelmingly positive experience I had plain and simple. If the Christian Church I knew was right, I'd have been cast in hell for all eternity!

Next I went back to my friend's house.

Before I went inside, I took a moment to feel the sun rise. I have yet to experience another sunrise like that one because I could actually "hear" and "feel" the sun rising and could see the sunbeams of energy coming toward the planet. I felt this energy wrap around my soul. That one sunrise inspired me greatly. To me it symbolized a sort of "rebirth" and a promise for our future.

In particular, I felt this new dawning day was going to be very special because I had great wonders to share, work to do, and the energy to do it all.

I felt the sense of purpose that I had been mistakenly searching for through the use of alcohol and drugs.

Now I actually loved myself, people and nature ... sober!

I felt peaceful, free, and extremely confident I could make it here on Gaia with new eyes to see this world. I had an optimistic outlook and knew I was blessed, and looking forward to sharing what happened with the souls closest to me.

Then I went inside the house by merely thinking myself inside. I had finally figured out that on Gaia I did not need to touch physical things like door-knobs until I inhabited a physical human body; I just passed right through the door to see my friends sleeping in the party room of the house.

There were five or six teens passed out on the floor. They were so darn cute! I saw my body there, too, still lying in the chair as I had left it. After all of the beauty and wonder I had seen, my body was not at all attractive to me. For without "me," my soul in it, my body had no purpose. It was simply the carrier of consciousness; my thoughts, feelings, and memories.

The true "me" was outside of my body, in what we call eternity, the magnetic space inside and outside of everything. My body was merely a container for my spirit to use while here walking on the surface of this planet.

More so, I knew what would happen when I got back in my body and I freely admit I did not want to lose my freedom and the love the spirit "me" felt then. I cringed as I knew my vibration would lessen and thereby my intense sense of being truly alive and functioning-fully would be sacrificed, again.

Although it was my deepest wish to remain bodiless, I willingly merged my spirit with my body which was lying asleep in the chair. In this lifetime, it was the hardest decision I had ever made. I awoke as soon as I rejoined it but much of the love and peace and confidence and positive feelings began to slowly melt away, just as I expected they would.

The absolute freedom of movement I felt a second ago was gone. I thought about going somewhere, but I felt really heavy and really slow now.

Nonetheless, I remembered everything that happened to me before, during, and after the experience. All of my body parts worked, and all of my senses worked. So all things considered, I was relieved to see my body had remained operational.

A twinge of excitement roused me as I wanted to share my story with my family and friends right away while it was still crystal-clear and fresh in my mind's eye.

Chapter 11

Afterward

"Who looks outside, dreams; who looks inside, awakes."
—Carl Jung

"You are not MY master," my friend Jack screamed.

In my enthusiasm, I woke up my friends to tell them what happened to me, specifically that a guardian angel named Bob told me I was a master-in-training. I started to tell them the part about me going to and waking up in a place that seemed to be from the very distant past or the future. They all just laughed at me and told me that I just overdosed on drugs and had a bad trip.

They said I was crazy!

None of them even wanted to hear what I was saying. The guys were all tired from a long night of partying and I had just awakened them at the crack of dawn babbling about Spirit City and what I am here to do for us all. They said I had just passed out in the chair all night because I overdosed on drugs and I didn't go anywhere and to stop talking crazy about it. I could see they were scared because of what I did tell them.

Specifically, I told them if the kind of trip I had were any indication of this drug's potential, it would indeed become very popular in the near future. They were not amused nor in a receptive mood.

I decided to leave.

I wasn't going to stay any longer and try to convince my friends of something they so obviously didn't want to contemplate, that we can exist outside our body in another realm in the sky.

Not one of my friends wanted to know anything about what happened to me. I could tell they were very scared, too, because I did almost die and that would have definitely created trouble for them with the law. In short, the time wasn't right for what I had to share.

Before I left the party house, I pulled out the bag of pot in my pocket and went over to the bar to retrieve my pack of cigarettes. Then without a second thought about the promises I made to change my lifestyle, I rolled a joint and smoked a cigarette as I did so. The all too familiar feelings of rejection and negative self-worth were beginning to consume me once again even at this early stage of return.

No doubt about it, I still had all of the problems here that I had before the otherworldly experience. I began to wonder how I could be of service to anyone, especially if nobody was going to believe me, and I couldn't conclusively prove what happened was real. My friends didn't believe me, and they were the ones I trusted the most at that time. Their initial reaction when I tried to share my story was a key factor in what I decided to do next.

My feelings had been hurt, and using childish logic, I decided that if my friends weren't going to believe me, and most of the rest of my life was still going to be tough, I would just pretend the whole thing never happened.

Already I regretted the decision I had made to return. I thought things would be magically different since I knew more about how the universe worked and everyone else would want to know these secrets too. Nope, that was clearly not the case.

Ignorance is indeed bliss evidently.

So I needed to change my orientation to this task and I wasn't ready yet. I also felt the vibrations of my friend's thoughts and a sense of pending danger if I stayed around these people.

I went home and tried to sleep but couldn't.

In fact, I ended up not sleeping well for the next two nights. I thought over what I'd experienced and tried to process it all and found out that I couldn't really. I had a very tough time making sense of it all, so I worked hard on convincing myself my friends were right. I simply overdosed and hallucinated and that was that folks—or so I wished.

To make matters worse, because of how my friends reacted, I could not even begin to think about telling my family about this fantastic journey through the world of spirit. I felt they would have me committed to a mental hospital. I mistrusted everyone except my guardian angel and now I was rejecting his counsel as well.

In fact, Bob returned to me in a dream the next night but I told him to bug off and have not seen him since. He wanted me to develop my psychic-type abilities further and I refused. I didn't want to know what was going to happen in the future, to me or anyone else. I had enough problems without seeing more to come.

Nonetheless, a few months later I did use my insights to remind one young friend several times that he needed to be extremely careful with his drinking and driving behavior. But he chose not to listen; even laughed at me about it, telling me to shut up and stop my "crazy talk."

He died later that summer in a car crash while driving drunk.

This incident affected me greatly; I now considered myself one really messed-up guy. I became very, very angry because I knew this automobile accident would result in a fatality and I couldn't prevent it. I was lacking the communication skills and confidence to get this important warning message heard by my beloved friend, and that made me feel awful.

Thus, in the early years, the last thing I ever wanted to think about was my near-death experience. I wanted to be normal and I sincerely regretted not drinking from the river of forgetfulness running through the heart of Spirit City when I had the chance. In hindsight, I can see how being oblivious to our spiritual origins and powers is a blessing.

Whatever the case, in those early weeks, I set out to find work with a vengeance. I got a job at a *Taco Bell* at first then a short time later I started working at factories. My idea of leaving the Detroit area fell by the wayside. I was very bitter about my whole NDE and set out to prove that I didn't need Bob or the wise group of counselors who had provided me with a guided life review in Spirit City.

For the most part, I felt the negativity again that this planet is steeped in constantly by thoughts and feelings that are counterproductive to well-being. It was the same bad vibration that I was trying to get away from in the first place and now it was going to be more of an influence than ever before I was sensing.

The truth is the problems I had in my life didn't magically go away like I half-expected they would and I had yet to grow the personality characteristics and leadership skills I needed to live a healthy, positive and productive lifestyle.

Plain and simple, I couldn't ignore the status quo that bound me to its confining self-limiting circumstances based upon its myopic belief systems; life was too big to handle by myself. I still didn't have the confidence to take my intuitions seriously and live on those terms. I also felt sad in my heart and a bit resentful because I chose to leave Spirit City to serve others here but they didn't want my help.

The bottom-line was I felt lonelier than ever before, more depressed than ever before, and more negative than ever before. I was in a real way, a stranger in a strange land.

Chapter 12

Today

"A mind stretched by a new idea
can never go back to its original dimensions."
—*Oliver Wendell Holmes*

Here I sit nearly thirty years later.

My life played out the same way I understood that it would based upon what I was shown by my guardian angel and group counselors in Spirit City.

I did have employment, money, and marriage problems.

All of the scenarios unfolded as they were supposed to happen despite all my attempts to change them. The last three decades have for certain been a painful albeit growing experience for me.

On the positive side, I can report that I eventually did overcome my depression and grew enough confidence to share this story and be a more positive person, but it took a long time! I still have my share of problems, but at least my experience is out in the open; it will not hurt me anymore.

Ultimately, I was prompted to explore the metaphysical bookstores where I discovered a host of published works that provided me with the confirmation I needed that I was not "crazy." Indeed, the more I read, the more I felt an urge to share my story with others, too.

The unvarnished truth is that I went to heaven, or at least one of them that is connected to Earth, and brought back the simple message to love one another.

Believe it or not, I feel strongly that this elemental philosophy is the largest "master" key to all that is going on both here and hereafter. Do not judge souls as worthy or not of your love: Love them unconditionally as life loves us and, yes, this is a major challenge for certain!

No doubt creation is perfect as it is designed; we just forget to keep our lives in balance with our heart's guidance and allow our minds to conjure incredible crises to confront.

So in that sense, we co-create reality—usually disasters!

Today I am glad to have had the opportunity to place my story in your hands and hearts because I feel better about it now myself. It is my hope that each person who reads my book will take away something of value that can be used in service to our war weary world.

In closing, it is my sincere prayer that once it is time for your own transition into the higher realms that you too will have a most rewarding *Journey Through the World of Spirit.*

Appendix A

The Q&A Session with David Oakford

Over the past thirty years, I haven't been able to answer all of the questions sent to me given the time constraints of my family and work responsibilities. Thus, I've selected a few of the more common concerns acknowledging that words alone will never replace direct personal "feeling" experiences of truth. I must assume then that this is why the great philosophers indeed counseled us: "Know Thyself." (Please see this website for updates on topics of concern: http://www.hometown.aol.com/oakfords/main.html)

Topic of Concern: Reincarnation

Q. Could you please shed light on the doctrine of reincarnation as was revealed to you?

A. First, I have to say that I am a firm believer in reincarnation based upon what I was shown as the goal of life: learning how to love unconditionally. In fact, I became completely aware of past lives when I was on the wooden bench awaiting my entrance into the group of beings for a life review evaluation. But I also saw flashes of other lives too. So for me the soul is a never ending cycle of consciousness that lives forever but incarnates again and again and again for one reason: service to creation. The purpose of these infinite lifetimes is to be of service to human and other beings as well as learn how to practice meaningful stewardship of natural resources that Gaia produces for us as we need them.

Topic of Concern: Spiritual Aftereffects

Q. Has the experience changed your faith and prayer life at all?

A. Before my experience I never really had a belief system, faith, or a prayer life. I still don't ascribe to any one faith. I just believe in what I was shown and being as loving and kind as I can. That in effect is my religion: kindness. I like certain aspects of all faiths, but I'm a little choosy in what I will or will not accept from them. What I do accept without hesitation is what best correlates with what I was shown. Nonetheless, I do have a prayer life. When I pray, I pray to the universe as a whole. I consider everything in the universe as an extension of God, so I pray to the whole thing. When I pray I try to pray for something good for someone else rather than anything for me. I figure that I'll see and feel it again later on.

Topic of Concern: Dreams, Visions, and Revelations

Q. Do you have any special visions or dreams of any sort since your visit?

A. I've had many cool dreams over the years, but nothing special like the NDE. But I feel dreams may well be tonight's answer to tomorrow's questions. I had these two dreams in 1997, just after I began to come forward with my revelations.

Here are examples:

One night, I dreamed I was walking in a field, a brown field. The sky was sunny and the earth was warm. With me were two other souls, an old man, and a young boy. We were walking. I looked ahead and saw a black beast in the distance. He was heading straight toward us. I pointed this out to the old man, and this creature dropped in its tracks.

The old man said: "Good! This is good .... now, you only have one left!" Next, the old man opened the book he was carrying and placed it on a stand so I could see it. The book had a map of the world marked with names of certain places, and dates; the old man told me these were where certain spirits are in the world.

Then I woke up.

Another dream:

I traveled to a big city, to see a friend who ran a house for disadvantaged people. I saw people there, each having their own problem with their bodies and minds. I wanted to help them. My friend told me to look out the window. I saw a part of the city raised up in the air. It was very beautiful and I could tell it was special. My friend said I needed to go there, they needed my help. I left the house and started walking toward the raised city. I started passing through a dangerous place of darkness. I could see the raised city still, but I came across obstacles along the way, dark alleys and bad neighborhoods. Someone even tried to attack me, but I bested him. The next one came and we started to battle.

Then I woke up.

Topic of Concern: Memory Recall of NDE and Dreams

Q. Why is it, in your opinion, that some people are allowed such "trips" into other realms in either true near-death situations, or in dreams, while others are not?

A. I'm not entirely sure but it may have something to do with not harming others by using my insights unwisely. For example: What would I do if I knew I was someone who hurt a lot of people in a previous life? I would think that would be dangerous for one to know. Why some remember and some don't I think would depend on their circumstances as an individual, and where they might be in the spiritual evolution cycle, which I have no way of knowing, of course. However, one thing I know about dreams is this: You can program yourself to remember them. I've done it. It takes a good and prolonged effort and an investment in self-programming meditation.

Topic of Concern: Ascended Masters

Q. I was born a Muslim and follow the teachings of Mohammed (peace be on him). I'm wondering why so many NDE's have been "guided" or touched in a sense by the prophet Jesus, while other prophets do not seem to be mentioned. Could it be due to the fact that, when we come to the Earth, (Gaia) we chose to be a certain religion, guided by a certain prophet and in turn it is that prophet that guides us back home?

A. I'm not sure why so many NDE's report seeing the great master Jesus and not other masters as a rule. Personally I believe God doesn't care what religion you are but whether you understand that the message is one of love. I saw a Jesus entity, but one example of many great world masters like Mohammed, and Buddha. More so, others that have had NDEs saw Jesus in a very different context than I did—and may very likely be based on their cultural background, thus creating a unique perception of him. You might be interested in this tidbit. According to the Islamic legend called "Miraj," the Prophet Mohammed had an experience that is similar in many respects to a near-death experience. He is said to have ascended to heaven to visit the seven heavens [and, in some accounts, the fires of hell] in the company of the archangel Gabriel. In the Koran, Muhammad's enemies are quoted as saying that they would not believe him unless he ascends to heaven and brings down a book (Sura 17:92-95).

Topic of Concern: Animal Spirits

Q. Can you refer me to material on animal spirits?

A. There is a lot of material about animal spirits on the Internet. Many cultures believe in animal spirits, especially the Native American culture. Shamans work with animal spirits and have done so for centuries, maybe even longer. Shamans can be found in all cultures. My favorite site about animal spirits is: "Shamanism: Working with Animal Spirits," (http://www. geocities.com/rainforest/4076/index1.html) but there are many more sites on the web you could check out.

Topic of Concern: Connecting to the Spirit World

Q. Do you practice any form of meditation and are you still able to connect with your Guardian Angel?

A. I meditate, but I do it in my own way, not any formal system to it really. My meditation consists of waking up at 5 a.m. most mornings on my own—no alarm clock—getting up for a minute, then back to bed and be in a type of "doldrums" until 7 a.m. That is, I am in a half-awake—half-dream state and that is what works for me, usually sets me in the right frame-of-mind for my day. And, yes, I feel a connection to Bob and know he is still here if I truly need him. I believe he manifests when I use my intuition for the most part. I don't hear his voice or anything now, but if I ask a question from the depth of my heart, an answer comes right away. Remember the four entities I met in the one building before I went for my life review? I believe they are now my children and I interact with them daily!

Topic of Concern: Astrology

Q. You've mentioned that you are a Leo. Do you feel there is truth in horoscopes, or does God direct our lives and give us direction? Do the stars have an impact on our decisions and control our destinies?

A. Yes, I feel there is some truth to horoscopes, but I think astrology in and of itself is a much bigger concept, especially in the afterlife. Astrology deals with the energies of the universe, the planets, the stars and those alignments. In my story, I mention the planets all have a specific theme for learning. All these themes center upon how to manage highly-charged emotions and feelings that our souls can use to meet the objectives of a given lifetime on a given planet. That is, life, death, and rebirth is about self-empowerment. Since I believe God is everywhere and everything, I have to say "He" does influence our lives, but we are the ones who have to make the final decisions. We have free will and I don't think our destinies are determined by the stars, rather I choose to believe we use the light energy within the stars and planets themselves to shape our own destinies lifetime-after-lifetime.

Topic of Concern: Gaia

Q. I'm just wondering why you came back with this particular message, while the greater percentage of NDE accounts do not say anything about Gaia.

A. In fact, I've spent a lot of time wondering about many aspects of my experience. To begin with: why me at all? Why doesn't my account match others? All good questions including why the Gaia name came up? But I'm not sure the name matters as much as the concepts presented do as to our treatment of nature. Most NDE's are described from a different angle because we each come from different backgrounds. Thus, our questions would be unique. I'm sure of one thing; this is a great planet whatever her name is!

Topic of Concern: Skeptics

Q. I was wondering what you thought about all this talk that scientists can "create" near-death experiences with drugs or touching parts of the brain? What's that all about? Are the experiences they are creating in laboratories anything in comparison to what you experienced? Is it possible that this is just some kind of chemical reaction taking place in the brain at the time of death? What are your answers to the questions of the skeptics?

A. Yes, I have read about one documented case of a man having an NDE, who then a week later had almost the same NDE after he was given the drug ketamine. Who knows what consciousness is made of for that matter? A psychiatrist at the University of New Mexico, Rick Strassman, M.D., has written a book that speculates that our minds are made of molecules! Accordingly, he titled his research *DMT: The Spirit Molecule*. My experience was triggered by what I'm sure was a massive shift of my body's chemistry. Clearly I can't discount the possibility the chemicals in the PCP created my experiences. In fact, I used that rationale to try to deal with my experience for a long time, to pack it up and put it away. It just didn't work. I freely admit I can't prove any of this beyond a reasonable doubt to anyone but me. But the drug angle does have its problems. The reason I don't think the drugs did it is that the entire event is coherent, it made sense to me then, and it still makes sense to me today. Sometimes I envy the skeptics because they have a choice to believe or not to believe. I simply don't have that luxury anymore. I am no longer innocent.

Topic of Concern: Reason for Delay in Sharing NDE

Q. I was wondering if it really took all these years to put your NDE into perspective or is it just time to tell it now?

A. Yes, my NDE occurred in the summer of 1979. Indeed I tried to tell my friends about it afterward, but they just said I was crazy. I didn't tell anyone for a long time after that because of that trauma. I did tell my wife about it, but not really the whole thing. To this day, I have never told the entire NDE all in one sitting. There are other reasons as well. Besides being considered crazy I likewise suppressed the experience because I already had a full plate. Recall I was a teenager. Also, I couldn't just walk up to someone in person and tell them how life, death, and rebirth work. That doesn't even work today!

In plain terms, you have to be ready to listen and learn!

Appendix B

The Complete Idiot's Guide to Near Death Experiences

by P.M.H. Atwater

Although the term "near-death experience" was coined as recently as the 1970's, these episodes have occurred and have been written about for thousands of years. Plato wrote of a near-death experience in the Republic. And in the Old Testament, there are repeated cautions to the Hebrew people against following the practices of their neighbors, who believed that the dead lived on and could be communicated with, calling such beliefs and activities "an abomination unto the Lord." It's understandable that death fascinates us; it's so much a part of everyday life. Here is an example from our modern times to illustrate the richness of the NDE itself:

In 1943, having contracted double pneumonia, 20-year-old U.S. Army private George Ritchie was pronounced dead, and his corpse was taken to the morgue. An orderly, however, thought he saw a movement from Ritchie's body. Ritchie's death was reconfirmed by the medical personnel, but the orderly insisted that he'd seen Ritchie's hand move. On the basis and conviction of the orderly's claim, adrenalin was injected into Ritchie, his vital signs returned, and he came back to life. Afterwards, Ritchie became a psychiatrist; often speaking of the extraordinary experiences he had while clinically considered dead.

The Moody Miracle

Then in 1965, an undergraduate philosophy student at the University of Virginia, Raymond Moody Jr. overheard Dr. Ritchie telling his story and became fascinated by it. But he didn't pursue it. Over the years, however, he heard other similar stories, the contents of which were nearly identical to that first account he'd heard as an undergraduate student. In 1972, Moody decided to enter medical school. By this time he had acquired a sizable number of accounts about people who had revived and returned to life with stories of an afterlife. Dr. Moody was encouraged to give public talks about what he called *near-death experiences*. In 1975, after becoming a medical doctor, he published an account of 150 stories he'd gathered in a landmark book titled *"Life After Life."*

The furor Moody's book elicited would never have packed the wallop it did were it not for social psychologist Kenneth Ring, Ph.D., a Professor at the University of Connecticut. He was so moved by the implications inherent in the NDE that he launched the first scientific study of the phenomenon. Five years later Ring was able to verify Moody's work in *"Life At Death,"* and in doing so opened-wide the floodgates to the serious inquiry that established that the near-death experience is no dream, vision, fairy tale, hallucination, or the product of anyone's imagination. It is a real event that happens to real people, regardless of their age, culture, education, or belief.

What is the Near Death Experience?

Near death states can occur when an individual brushes death, almost dies, or is pronounced clinically dead, yet later revives or is resuscitated. Typically, the near-death experiencers (NDErs) register neither pulse nor breath for an average of 10 to 15 minutes. It's not unusual to hear of those who were dead for over an hour.

Regardless of how long the experiences last, though, NDE episodes are significant in that they remain lucid and coherent in the experiencer's mind over time. These experiences happen to anyone at any age, including newborns and infants.

U.S. News & World Report's March 1997 poll estimated that 15 million Americans have had a near-death experience, or roughly one-third of those who are at death's door. But this survey only addresses adult experiencers.

In his ground-breaking study of child experiencers done in the late 1980's, Melvin Morse, M.D., author of *Closer to the Light* estimates that among children close to death, around 70 percent have had a near-death experience.

NDEs can range in content from an out-of-body experience to being in the presence of God. They imply that there may be life after death because of the imagery encountered and the accuracy of details that often could not have been known by the experiencer in advance.

Common Elements in Near-Death Scenarios

Thousands of near-death *scenarios* have now been studied worldwide revealing common elements, even though the actual way the various elements are experienced and described may vary widely. Some people report finding themselves in a garden, walking along a road, or skipping through a pasture. Others describe great cities that sparkle like jewels or what it's like to hop aboard a light ray for a trip through the universe. Many speak of entering huge libraries or halls of judgment, while a large number wind up in a familiar terrain talking with deceased loved ones or playing with former pets that act just like they did while they were alive. Religious figures such as Jesus or Buddha, angels of various persuasions, beings of light, and spiritual guardians of every sort are reported so often they have become the mainstay of near-death literature. Dr. Moody's original work identified 15 elements overall:

- Ineffability, beyond the limits of any language to describe
- Hearing yourself pronounced dead
- Feelings of peace and quiet
- Hearing unusual noises

- Seeing a dark tunnel
- Finding yourself outside your body
- Meeting "spiritual beings"
- A very bright light experienced as a "being of light"
- A panoramic life review
- Sensing a border or limit to where you can go
- Coming back into your body
- Frustrating attempts to tell others about what happened to you
- Subtle "broadening and deepening" of your life afterward
- Elimination of the fear of death
- Corroboration of events witnessed while out of your body

Two years later, after hundreds of interviews, Moody added four more elements to his list of common components to what experiencers claim to have encountered:

- A realm where all knowledge exists
- Cities of light
- A realm of bewildered spirits
- Supernatural rescues

Let's focus on this last element for a moment.

Many near-death experiencers report experiencing what have come to be called supernatural rescues. These are occurrences in which the person benefits physically from "heavenly" intervention, as in having tumors disappear or a "physical," detached hand that suddenly appears from out of nowhere to pull the person to safety.

As more research was done, other professionals noted that near-death states could also include features besides the mystical, such as depersonal elements and *hyper alertness.*

Tripping Through the Tunnel

Some NDErs mention traveling through a tunnel as part of their near-death scenario. Some refer to this tunnel as long and dark and that they were alone in it throughout their journey. Others say there were bright lights that flashed along its walls, or that it was colored or even transparent, and that other people were there. Almost everyone states that they swooshed through at great speed. Some said they heard and felt the sensation of wind rushing by them. Just as many said the tunnel went up, as down, or straight.

In most cases, a light appears at the end of the tunnel, and experiencers note that is where they are headed—a light described as brighter than the sun that doesn't hurt their eyes if they look at it. This light is invariably as loving, intelligent, accepting, forgiving, and ever so wonderful as it can be.

The Birth of a Controversy

It's important to take a closer look at some of the near-death scenarios, and now we'll explain why. The truth is that despite popular views and dramatizations, seldom will any near-death experiencer's scenario contain all the elements that have been noted so far and commonly cited as "typical." Indeed, the average experience will consist of about half of them.

The famed "tunnel" component, for example, is present in less than one-third of the actual experiences. In the first-ever national poll taken on near-death states by Gallup in 1982, only 9 percent claimed to have passed through a tunnel. But the image is nonetheless so captivating and popularized that many NDErs make up a tunnel component to their episode, just so they can convince themselves that what happened to them was genuine!

In short, the now-popular notion that *all* experiencers leave their bodies, go through a tunnel into the light, meet deceased relatives in heaven, and are then told to come back, is fanciful at best and confusing at the worst. They can mislead not only the general public but the experiencers as well.

Excluded almost entirely from the public are unpleasant or hellish scenes, feelings of distress, threatening beings, flashes of light and dark, complicated and lengthy involvement with otherworldly teachers, ongoing experiments with matter and creation, short trips that seem to have little meaning, disembodied voices, historical backgrounds and so forth. These are as much a part of many individuals' near-death states as are the more familiar elements.

The "alarm bell" regarding the confusion about what constituted a "true" near-death experience and what didn't was ultimately sounded by the health-care community. They were trying to train medical personnel on how to recognize if a patient might be in the process of having or might have just had a near-death experience. What they had to go on was the "universal model" that, as we've seen, wasn't proving to be very helpful As a result, the standards the medical community was hoping to provide proved not to exist.

Then Bruce Greyson, M.D., in an effort to achieve consensus, contacted all the top researchers of near-death states by letter and said, in essence, that the time has come when we must have common criteria that the health care community can use and, for that matter, anyone else. The following way of dividing the near-death experience into two categories of "context of experience" and "content of experience" was suggested in Greyson's letter.

The context of experience was defined as containing one or both of the following two elements: 1) "Symptoms or signs suggestive of death, or of serious medical illness, injury, or physiological crisis/accident of some kind, and/or 2) The experiencer's expectation or sense of imminent death."

The content of experience was defined as "an intense awareness, sense, or experience of 'other worldliness,' whether pleasant or unpleasant, strange or ecstatic. The episode can be brief or can be lengthy and consist of multiple elements."

The most common elements are listed below:

- Visualizing or experiencing being apart from the physical body, perhaps with the ability to change locations
- Greatly enhanced cognition (thoughts clear, rapid, and hyper-lucid)
- A darkness or light that is perceived as alive and intelligent and powerful
- Sense of a presence
- Sensations of movement (one's own or things around oneself)
- Hyper-alert faculties (heightened sense of smell, taste, touch, sight, and sound)
- Sudden overwhelming floods of emotion or feelings
- Encounter with an identified deceased person or animal or seemingly non-physical entity
- Life review (like a movie or in segments, or a direct intense reliving)
- Information can be imparted, perhaps dialogue takes place

Contemporary medical procedures make it possible to survive clinical death in many cases. Those who have done so have come back to tell us tales that we still don't quite understand, but that inspire us and challenge our understanding of life as well as death itself.

Problems in Communication

As I continued my research, I came to realize that it wasn't the experience per se that made the biggest difference, but rather, how the individual felt and talked about it. And talking about communicating the experience was itself often part of the problem in trying to understand not only the meaning but also the nature of a near-death experience.

The Language Barrier

Near-death experiences are fundamentally ineffable beyond the limits to be adequately described by language. Adults struggle for the right words to use, and never quite seem to find any combination that really works to help them get their point across. So, you can imagine, therefore, that if adult experiencers find the constraints of language a barrier, child experiencers struggle even more so to find the right words.

I have come to believe this problem of finding the "right words" to describe one's experience is the major reason why so many experiencers fall back on simply painting the kind of word picture they feel they can most easily convey to others. Remember, after all, the experience itself is startlingly unique, and many discount it. There's safety in numbers: You're not as apt to be labeled "a nut" if you describe your experience in language typical to that of your family, religion, or society.

Embarrassed Into Secrecy

Seldom do experiencers return with their lifelong beliefs still intact. Invariably, the beliefs are challenged or stretched beyond what was once normal or typical for the person. This can be both good and not so good, depending on the individual involved. One woman, who was a minister's wife, told me she could no longer attend church and listen to her husband's sermons afterward. "What he's telling the congregation is wrong. I know better, I was there, and God doesn't ask that of us."

Just as with everyday life, in near-death states, if what you experience runs counter to—or even completely contradicts—your previous beliefs or upbringing, it won't necessarily be a language problem that keeps you from sharing your experience. It could be embarrassment or suddenly feeling "out of synch" with the world around you. Additionally, out of shame, or for a million other reasons, an experiencer may not want to admit to others that his or her experience was hellish instead of heavenly.

THE FOUR TYPES OF NEAR-DEATH EXPERIENCES

1. *Initial experience* (sometimes referred to as the" non-experience").

Involves elements such as a loving nothingness, the living dark, a friendly voice, a brief out of body experience, or a manifestation of some type. Usually experienced by those who seem to need the least amount of evidence for proof of survival, or who need the least amount of shake-up in their lives at that point in time. Often, this becomes a "seed" experience or an introduction to other ways of perceiving and recognizing reality.

Incident rate:

76 percent with child experiencers

20 percent with adult experiencers

2. *Unpleasant and/or Hell-Like Experience* (inner cleansing and self-confrontation),

Encounter with a threatening void, stark limbo, or hellish purgatory, or scenes of a startling and unexpected indifference (like being shunned), even "hauntings" from one's own past. Usually experienced by those who seem to have deeply suppressed or repressed guilt, fear, and anger, and/or those who expect some kind of punishment or discomfort after death.

Incident rate:

3 percent with child experiencers

15 percent with adult experiencers

3. *Pleasant and/or Heaven-Like Experience* (reassurance and self-validation).

Heaven-like scenarios of loving family reunions with those who have died previously, reassuring religious figures or light beings, validation that life counts, affirmative and inspiring dialogue. Usually experienced by those who most need to know how loved they are and how important life is and how every effort has a purpose in the overall scheme of things.

Incident rate:

19 percent with child experiencers

47 percent with adult experiencers

4. *Transcendent Experience* (expansive revelations, alternate realities).

Exposure to otherworldly dimensions and scenes beyond the individual's frame of reference; sometimes includes revelations of greater truths. Seldom personal in content. Usually experienced by those who are ready for a "mind stretching" challenge and/or individuals who are more apt to use (to whatever degree) the truths that are revealed to them.

Incident rate:

2 percent with child experiencers

18 percent with adult experiencers

Major Characteristics Displayed by People Who Have Undergone Near-Death Experiences

Psychological

Loss of a fear of death, more spiritual—less religious, abstract easily, philosophical, can go through bouts of depression, disregard for time, more generous and charitable, form expansive concepts of love while at the same time challenged to initiate and maintain satisfying relationships, "inner child" issues exaggerated, less competitive, convinced of life's purpose, rejection of previous limitations and norms, heightened sense of taste-touch-texture-smell, increased psychic ability and future memory episodes, charismatic, childlike sense of wonder and joy, less stressed, more detached and objective (disassociation), "merge" easily (absorption), hunger for knowledge and learning.

Physiological

Changes in thought processing (switch from sequential/selective thinking and an acceptance of ambiguity), insatiable curiosity, heightened intelligence, more creative and inventive, unusual sensitivity to light and sound, substantially more or less energy (even energy surges, often more sexual), reversal of body clock, lower blood pressure, accelerated metabolic and substance absorption rates (decreased tolerance of pharmaceuticals and chemically treated products), electrical sensitivity, synethesia (multiple sensing), increased allergies or sensitivities, a preference for less meat and more vegetables and grains, physically younger looking (before and after photos can differ)

Not everyone exhibits all of these characteristic aftereffects certainly, but in fact the majority do. Whichever traits do appear can be brand new or expansions or enlargements of abilities already present within the experiencer (latent skills).

After a near-death experience, challenges come quickly. Confusion and misunderstanding stack up; changes are continuous. The whole drama may seem like the "luck of the draw" or simply "the way things are," until the experiencer begins to read research findings and talk to others who have had the same experience. Then "connecting the dots" is possible. It's always a surprise to realize just how much this particular phenomenon can alter you and the way you live your life—perhaps permanently.

Near-death states initially startle, then overwhelm experiencers of any age. How long these episodes remain active in their memory has a lot to do with the intensity of their impact and the degree to which details can be verified. Any thought that these states are dreams is utterly shattered once an experiencer is able to link what he or she has witnessed while "dead" with what later proves to be true. The shock of these observations or revelations—that could not have been known in advance—leaves an indelible imprint on the individual's mind. Even if no such connection between subjective experience and subsequent reality is ever made, intensity alone packs a big wallop.

Typical adult experiencers respond to this intensity by giving it their full attention. They tend to relive what happened again and again in their struggle to assess whatever meaning and value the event might have for them. The quest to understand demands they search for explanations, and they do so with passion. For some, this need becomes a driving force that pushes them over and above the experience itself into making the kind of changes in their life that correspond to what they feel their episodes to mean. Notice I said, "feel." Pretend you're the near-death experiencer; this is what you must consider:

• *Accepting means taking a risk.* To accept my experience and integrate it into my daily life might well mean ridicule and scorn from others, and having to confront the issue of insanity again and again. I could be labeled undesirable or fake because I have no proof to offer, or, I could be accused of trying to be some kind of holy seer or divine prophet. Acceptance would change my life completely, necessitating that I live what I know to be true. Since my experience challenged the validity of everything I have previously known, accepting it would mean I would have to relearn and redefine life, possibly from scratch. This means I could lose a lot. I could also gain. I could gain everything and everyone, and possibly learn how to grow closer to god.

- *Rejecting means denial.* To reject having had the experience would mean not only denying it occurred, but my own sense of integrity, honesty, and inner truth. Rejection would mean turning my back on what I know happened and pretending it away. But it would also mean I would have to take fewer risks and could retain what security and comfort I still possess. Rejection would be sensible and practical, all things considered, allowing me more time to concentrate on healing and the continuance of life as usual. No one would ever know the difference. There would be no further damage to my reputation or further insult to my family. My job and lifestyle would be preserved. But rejection would also mean I would have to deny what might been a peek at God, and the opportunity to experience divine oneness and truth. It would mean saying no when deep down inside I want to say yes.

They're Not Hallucinations

There are numerous medical conditions that can cause a sudden loss of consciousness that produce hallucinations. One of them is *syncope.*

Experiments have been done with healthy young adults, through the use of techniques such as hyperventilation, to create syncopal hallucinations. The result: Internal perceptions of colors and lights intensify to a glaring brightness; familiar people and landscapes are seen but seldom with detailed features; out of body views are from a height looking down; sounds range from roaring noises to screaming and unintelligible voices.

Seem familiar? Well, sort of. What's missing from these syncopal hallucinations, among other things, is the rich and vivid detail found in near-death states, along with the many independent verifications or what is seen, heard, smelled, or experienced by the individual that he or she could not have otherwise known.

The Evergreen Study

Known by its shortened name–the Evergreen Study–the proper title, as published in *Anabiosis–The Journal for Near-Death Studies*, is "Near-Death Experiences in a Pacific-Northwest American Population: The Evergreen Study." While we associate the Pacific Northwest with a logging country, the "Evergreen" in the title actually refers to Evergreen State College in Olympia, Washington, where the study was conducted over a five-month period, beginning in January 1981. Researchers are James H. Lindley, Sethryn Bryan, and Bob Conley. Forty-nine people who had 55 encounters with death are included in the study.

The researchers designed their investigation around the five stages of the near-death experience that Raymond Moody and Kenneth Ring identified:

1. A feeling of overwhelming peace
2. An out-of-body experience
3. Entrance into a dark tunnel or just darkness
4. Encountering a light
5. Entering the light

As had Drs. Moody and Ring, the researchers noted that these five stages are not experienced by every individual, nor should they be thought of as "consecutive levels." The fifth stage proved troublesome, as it implied that experiencers not only saw a light, but entered into it. Stage 5 also carried the meaning that within this light were "worlds" from which the light origi-nated. The researchers received no report confirming this. Instead, the light seemed to be non-physical; and if anything, the "worlds" had their origin in the light, not vice versa. They suggested renaming the fifth stage "the inner setting"–"a location of great natural beauty such as a garden, valley or meadow." This "inner setting" was where the experiencer spent time before deciding whether or not to return.

Following are the results obtained from those in the study:

1. 74.5 percent experienced Stage 1 (serenity)
2. 70.9 percent experienced Stage 2 (out-of-body experience)
3. 38.2 percent experienced Stage 3 (tunnel or darkness)
4. 56.4 percent experienced Stage 4 (seeing a light)
5. 34.5 percent experienced Stage 5 (entering an "inner setting")

Interestingly, during this early phase of inquiry into the phenomenon, the researchers found that 20 percent of the experiencers had accounts of "hellish" experiences—an episode type not mentioned in early books or articles–which the researchers defined as "one that contains extreme fear, panic, or anger."

Typically, they said, it "begins with a rush of fear and panic or with a vision of wrathful or fearful creatures." Negative aspects often changed to positive ones, though, during the episode.

They also found that it was common for unpleasant sensations to come at the end of a positive experience, suggesting to them a "fall from grace" as the individual returns from otherworldly tranquility to ordinary consciousness. Many experiencers supported this assumption by admitting that they didn't want to return and fought back.

Finally, the researchers made the intriguing suggestion that Stage 1—a feeling of peace—has a biological origin. At the onset of death and the breakdown of vital systems, the hypothalamus might release morphine-like substances (for example, endorphins) into our brains as a final biological attempt to produce a state of well-being. They found no biological basis for the remaining stages, however.

The Southern California Study

Published in *Anabiosis – The Journal for Near-Death Studies* in 1983 and formally known as "Near-Death Experiences in a Southern California Population," this study was conducted by J. Timothy Green and Penelope Friedman. It took place at California State University, Northridge, and consisted of in-depth interviews of 41 persons having had a total of 50 near-death experiences.

Beginning in January and concluding in December 1981, the researchers placed ads in various Los Angeles area newspapers asking to interview "persons who have been close to death or clinically dead." It was only after inquiries were received that the researchers revealed their deeper concerns: Had the person "had an experience while unconscious"? By initially withholding their true intention, they had also hoped to arrive at better percentages across the board of people who were once at death's door and survived.

As with the Evergreen Study, the Southern California Study examined reports in terms of the Moody/Ring stages. Here are the results:

- 70 percent experienced Stage 1.
- 66 percent experienced Stage 2.
- 32 percent experienced Stage 3.
- 62 percent experienced Stage 4.
- 18 percent experienced Stage 5

In addition, 48 percent of the respondents said they encountered spirit beings, deceased friends or relatives, or religious figures; and 12 percent had a life review. Ninety-six percent considered the experience was unlike anything they'd ever had in a dream.

To sum this all up, the researchers of the Southern California Study suggested that rather than contradicting or undermining science, this newly discovered human experience "extends rather than refutes what we already know much in the same way that Einstein's view of the universe extended Newton's." They observed that: "The implications the near-death experience presents … are potentially so revolutionary that at this point in history, when mankind has harnessed enough energy to destroy itself many times over, a deeper understanding of ourselves and our continuum might be crucial."

About the Author

P.M.H. Atwater Lh.D. is one of the original researchers of the near-death phenomenon, having begun her work in 1978 after experiencing three near-death episodes. Her research contains the largest database to date on near-death experiencers, and her contribution to the field is widely acknowledged. The International Association of Near-Death Studies considers her books *Coming Back to Life* and *Beyond the Light* bibles of the near-death experience; *Children of the New Millennium* is a must read. In her book *Future Memory* she expanded her work into areas of brain development that call for a reconsideration of what is presently known about transformations of consciousness in general and the near-death phenomenon in particular.

P. M. H. Atwater has appeared on *Larry King Live, Regis and Kathi Lee, and Geraldo,* and is a workshop leader at major spiritual/holistic study retreats. She has been a speaker at International Association of Near Death Studies conferences, as well as the United Nations.

She lives in Charlottesville, Virginia, with her husband, Terry Young Atwater. More information can be found at: www.pmhatwater.com

Appendix C

Tranceformers: Shamans of the 21st Century

by John Jay Harper

Time is the substance from which I am made. Time is a river that carries me along, but I am the river; it is a tiger that devours me, but I am the tiger; it is a fire that consumes me, but I am the fire.—Jorge Luis Borges

The story you are about to read is true.

"John," the voice on the phone said, "I have some very bad news."

My best friend George Sebastian Viguet III (pronounced "Vee-gay") had died that day of a massive heart attack in Huntsville, Alabama, his wife had just informed me.

Born in White Castle, Louisiana on January 24th, 1947, he was a vibrant, young man of 40 when his life ended suddenly that Monday morning at 9:30 A.M. on November 9th, 1987, as officially noted on the Certificate of Death.

In fact, George drew his last breath in the medical clinic of his family physician located right next door to Huntsville Hospital. So you couldn't ask for a better location to have a cardiac crisis nor a better set of circumstances. That is, as I learned he drove himself there on the way to his office because he was not feeling well. He had hoped to merely get some medicine and be on his way again.

However as fate would have it, that was not in the cards for while being examined by the family doctor the worst possible scenario unfolded; his heart suddenly exploded. Thus all attempts to resuscitate him failed.

I had known George for 18 years.

We had met in 1969 as soldiers stationed at the U.S. Army Missile and Munitions Center and School, Redstone Arsenal, Alabama. Along with a few dozen other men undergoing highly-specialized training in computers, electronics, and missilery, we were assigned to the same select military unit, the 116th Ordnance Detachment that had transferred from Fort Riley, Kansas.

Our specific outfit was preparing for deployment as a one-of-a-kind missile support team to West Germany at the apex of the Cold War. Interestingly enough, we were going to set-up our shop at one of Adolph Hitler's former Nazi SS strongholds during WWII. It was called Merrell Barracks now.

Indeed I was really looking forward to this "field trip" of sorts, too, as I had studied the German language, culture, and history for 3 years while at Central Kitsap High School in Silverdale, Washington. Upon hindsight, or a past-life memory, it was as if I knew subconsciously that I was going to use that knowledge, again.

From Grits and Gravy to Bratwurst and Beer

The day to depart for Germany arrived and I awoke at the crack of dawn on January 28th, 1970, showered, shaved, dressed, breakfasted, and drove us to the Huntsville International Airport. Shortly thereafter, I kissed my wife of 2 months, Connie, goodbye as we watched our married officers and senior enlisted personnel get aboard our plane with their families, then the rest of us, for the flight's first leg to Philadelphia, Pennsylvania.

Upon arrival there we were taken by bus to McGuire Air Force Base, New Jersey, flying on then later that evening to Europe via the Military Airlift

Command (MAC).

Going overseas on a military assignment is a gut-wrenching experience. There is no greater trauma to a young, newly-married soldier especially than to be involuntarily torn from your loved ones' arms, in my opinion. A civilian has not a clue how difficult a task that is to do. So, of course, that day is forever etched into my mind and heart some 35-years later.

The shock is cultural, climatic, and culinary as well. For example, we departed Alabama on a warm clear-blue sky day and arrived in Germany on a cold, cloudy-rainy day at Rhein-Main Air Force Base in Frankfurt.

I went from "see ya'll later," to "Guten Tag!" I also went from an Alabama breakfast of "biscuits, grits, gravy, and coffee" to a German lunch of "bread, bratwurst, sauerkraut, and beer" in 24 hours!

Notwithstanding, we were gratefully bussed down to Nuernberg a few hours to the southeast along the Czechoslovakia border, finally settling into our new living quarters at Merrell Barracks late that evening totally exhausted.

I slept like the proverbial log that night oblivious to my stark surroundings. But in the morning I awoke to find myself within a massive, multi-story concrete block structure with bullet-holes visible on the walls.

These combat remnants we learned were the calling cards left behind by Allied GIs who captured it from the former Nazi SS occupants in 1945. No doubt if we were in the USA's fashionable mind-set today, we would have seen this sign displayed on a soldier's door somewhere: "Martha Stewart Does Not Live Here!" Whatever the case, the single guys were stuck here for the duration of their tour of duty.

In contrast, we married guys began counting the days until our wives would arrive "in country," so we could live downtown like German civilians. I wanted out of here as soon as possible as I did not fit in with this foot-loose and fancy-free single crowd at all anymore.

To digress a moment, George married Kathy, and I, Connie, a couple months before we had to ship out and so those days of separation were tortuous for us as I recall. But our wives arrived on April 10th, 1970 on a chartered flight out of New York City, and we made up for that lost time in a big way—visiting medieval castles among other things.

Specifically, Connie and I took an American Express Tour of Bavaria, Switzerland, the French Riviera, and northern Italy. In particular we attended the 1970 Grand Prix of Monaco, watching it from a hillside overlooking the harbor was surreal. Wow, what a day for the diary!

We likewise partied in our local German villages at every opportunity. A smile comes to my face as I recall us swaying back and forth with our liter-sized beer steins in synch to the native music being played in those big circus-like tents at the Folks Festivals.

I loved the yodeling songs and the spirited "Chicken Dance" and the food that added so much joy to these celebrations. These are fond memories for a big eater like me but they ended abruptly on May 7th, 1971 to be exact.

For Connie and I returned to Alabama, where her parents lived and I was accepted to attend the University of Alabama in Huntsville under the GI Bill, as did George and Kathy a few months later by the way.

Initially I began my collegiate studies in electronics engineering but George, on the other hand, pursued a rigorous curriculum in physics, graduating with honors. This guy was born to be a scientist: He was very bright and very introverted.

In fact, I was one of the few persons George felt comfortable talking to about non-technical matters, conversations held late at night usually over cold beer and hotly contested chess games. From these exchanges, I knew that George believed that when you were dead, you were dead and gone, period. That was it, game over.

But that was not my belief and at his elaborate Catholic funeral, where I was a pallbearer, I stared at that metal-box in front of me solemnly. I kept asking myself over and over again: Where is George?

Where in the world—or out of this world—is the "soul" of George right now at this very minute? I sincerely wanted to know the truth. This desperate heartfelt plea paid dividends, as George was not dead!

Talking Telepathically with the Dead

How do I know this is true? It is because in June 1988, nearly seven months to the day after I helped place his casket in a marble-faced mausoleum in Huntsville, Alabama, I saw George in my master bedroom in my new home in Silverdale, Washington, 2500 miles away from where he "died."

From indeed what I thought at first was merely a lucid dream of him, I saw George standing there shimmering in a holographic body of light right in front of me looking well—and smiling!

Although, initially, it was his clothing that really got my undivided attention because George was wearing a brightly-colored, short-sleeved Hawaiian luau shirt with a white beachcomber hat on his head. This was no dream and I stared at my friend like a deer caught in halogen headlights.

This is ironic, I mumbled. Here I quit my job in Alabama and moved back to my former hometown, Silverdale, in April of 1988 to get over the grief that I was experiencing: Yet there George stood, plain as the nose on his face!

George was really alive and now I had to deal with it. That was the tough part as my paradigm—model of reality—clearly did not include an option for talking to the dead, even if we did survive death itself. What about going to heaven and all that jazz; why would he remain and how could I see him now? Well, I was a science guy by training and temperament, too, so I started to slowly piece the psychological and physiological facts together.

This much I knew then: I had been in an altered state of mind, what I know now we call all too casually the state of "trance," when I saw him. That is, suddenly I could see multi-dimensionally and communicate telepathically with George. But one of the most bizarre aspects to my experience actually helped me validate it later as a bon a fide after-death communication.

That is, I saw that George had a row of flattened metal beer cans stuffed inside his hat's headband. Now we were both avid beer drinkers at the time of his "death," so that in and of itself was not surprising, yet upon deep reflection I grasped the significance to this comical imagery.

And this is what ultimately blew my mind—and third eye—wide open: Months later I recollected what I had said to George while at the funeral home in Huntsville, Alabama, not aloud but to myself. I had leaned over his casket to look him squarely in the face and then projected this thought attempting to alleviate the severity of the situation—at least for me. I said mentally to him, "George, a joke is a joke, let's go get a beer!"

To the point: George had heard me speak those words to him that day no doubt about it! Unequivocally, he was showing me symbolically by his colorful party attire and "the old beer cans in the hat band trick" that he was still very much alive and, equally, he was giving me a clue as to our own future psychic powers once we too reopen our third eye in era-2012.

Today I realize that mind-to-mind communication—telepathy—will become the common means of information exchange between the living and the "dead" in the years ahead, as well as with other so-called "alien" species within our living cosmos. This ability is not an anomaly, in other words, but is sine qua non of the mystic, prophet, and shaman-in-training as well.

In summary, it is simply part of the total psychic package of new tools that comes unwrapped when your third eye opens and you finally see into the Fifth Dimension. Thus I conclude as did science writer Lynne McTaggart of London, England in *The Field: The Quest for the Secret Force of the Universe*: "Death may be merely a matter of going home or, perhaps, staying behind—returning to The Field."

There is a fifth dimension beyond that which is known to man. It is a dimension as vast as space and as timeless as infinity. This is the home of our imagination.—Rod Serling (1924-1975), The Twilight Zone

About the Author

Dr. John Jay Harper is a clinical hypnotherapist and author of *Tranceformers: Shamans of the 21st Century*. He and his wife, Connie, live in Spokane, Washington and will soon be relocating to the Village on Sewanee Creek, Tennessee. For more information, please see www.johnjayharper.com

References

Antonette, J. Whispers of the Soul. J. Antonette, 1998.

Atwater, P. Beyond the Light, Morrow. William & Co., 1995.

Atwater, P. Children of the New Millennium.
Crown Publishing Group, 1999.

Atwater, P. with David H. Morgan. The Complete Idiot's Guide to Near-
Death Experiences. Macmillan USA, Inc. 2000.

Atwater P., and Joseph Chilton Pearce. The New Children and Near Death
Experiences. Bear and Company, 2003.

Atwater, P. We Live Forever: The Real Truth About Death. ARE Press, 2003.

Bailey, Lee Worth. The Near-Death Experience: A Reader. Routledge, 1996.

Bennett, Rita. To Heaven and Back. Zondervan Publishing House, 1997.

Berman, Philip L. The Journey Home. Simon & Schuster Trade, 1996.

Brinkley, Dannion, with Paul Perry. Saved by the Light.
HarperCollins Publishers, Inc, 1995.

Brubaker, Don. Absent from the Body. Peninsula Publishing, 1995.

Bubulka, Grace. Beyond this Reality. Word Dancer Press, 1994.

Cornford, Francis. The Republic of Plato. Oxford, 1945.

Dennis, Lynnclaire. The Pattern. Integral Publishing, 1997.

Dougherty, Ned. Fast Lane to Heaven.
Hampton Roads Publishing Co., Inc, 2001.

Duval, Matthew J. My Last Breath. PublishAmerica , 2003.

Eadie, Betty. Embraced by the Light. Bantam Books, Inc., 1994.

Eby, Richard. Caught up into Paradise. Baker Books, 1984.

Farr, Sidney Saylor. What Tom Sawyer Learned from Dying.
Hampton Roads Publishing Co., Inc., 1993.

Fenimore, Angie. Beyond the Darkness. Bantam Books, Inc., 1996.

Fowler, Raymond E. The Andreasson Affair: Phase Two,
Wild Flower Press, 1994.

Gibson, Arvin S. Fingerprints of God.
Horizon Publishers & Distributors, Inc., 1999.

Gibson, Arvin S., Journeys Beyond Life, Horizon Publishers, 1994.

Hagin, Kenneth E. I Believe in Visions.
   Faith Library Publications, Inc., 1984.

Harper, John Jay. Tranceformers: Shamans of the 21st Century. CA:
   Reality Press, 2006. See www.johnjayharper.com and
   www.reality-entertainment.com

Jung, Carl Gustav. Memories, Dreams, Reflections. Vintage Books, 1989.

Kubler-Ross. Elisabeth. One Life After Death. Celestial Arts, 1991.

Martin, Laurelynn. Searching for Home. 1996.

Moody. Jr, Raymond A. The Last Laugh.
   Hampton Roads Publishing Co, Inc. 1999.

Moody Jr. Raymond A. Life After Life. Harper San Francisco, 2001.

Morrissey, Dianne. You Can See the Light. Stillpoint Publishing, 1997.

Morse, Donald R. Searching for Eternity. Eagle Wing Books, Inc., 2000.

Neihardt, John G. Black Elk Speaks. University of Nebraska Press, 1989.

Newton, Michael. Journey of Souls. Llewellyn, 2002 .

Oakford, David. Soul Bared; a Metaphysical Journey.
   Publish America, 2004.

Piper, Don. 90 Minutes in Heaven. Revell, 2004.

Plato, The Republic, Penguin USA, 1976.

Price, Jan. The Other Side of Death. Ballantine Books, Inc., 1996.

Ring, Kenneth, with Evelyn E. Valarino. Lessons from the Light.
   Perseus Publishing, 1998.

Ring, Kenneth. Lessons From the Light: What We Can Learn From the
   Near Death Experience, Moment Point Press, 2006.

Ritchie, George G., with Elizabeth Sherrill. Return from Tomorrow.
   Revell, Fleming H. Company, 1983.

Ritchie, Jean. Deaths Door. Dell Publishing Company, Inc., 1996.

Rogers, Sandra H. Lessons from the Light. Warner Books, Inc., 1995.

Rosenblit, Daniel. Transformed by the Light. 1998.

Sabom, Michael B. Light and Death. Zondervan Publishing House, 1998.

Schwartz, Gary E. The Afterlife Experiments: Breakthrough Evidence
   of Life After Death. Altria, 2003.

Sharp, Kimberly Clark. After the Light. Authors Choice Press, 2003.

Storm, Howard. My Descent into Death. A Second Chance at Life
  Doubleday, 2005.
Sugrue, Thomas. There is a River: The Story of Edgar Cayce.
  A. R. E. Press, 1990.
Wallace, RaNelle, with Curtis Taylor. The Burning Within.
  Gold Leaf Press, 1994.
Williams, Kevin. Nothing Better Than Death. Xlibris, 2002.
Yensen, Arthur E. "I Saw Heaven", 1979, C/O Eric Yensen, 3407
  Fair Oaks Circle, Caldwell, Idaho 83605.

About The Author

David was born in 1959, in the shadow of the great auto plants in Warren, Michigan. He grew up on the "South Side" of town, on the Detroit border; which was, and still is, a great place to get into trouble! By the time he was 19 he was in some very dark times, which led up to his near death experience. After his experience he settled down and got a job as a crane operator at a machine tool plant. He made new friends and met the woman who eventually became his wife. He was laid off in 1982, a casualty of the manufacturing decline the Detroit area experienced in the early 1980's. During this time he tried very hard to forget his experience.

David spent five years in the US Navy from 1985-1990, operating the tactical data system, the radars and the missile launcher on the guided missile frigate USS Halyburton FFG-40. He also controlled helicopters that hunted submarines. This made him remember some of the aspects of the experience, but he still tried to forget what he had learned.

After his enlistment ended he earned a Bachelor of Business Administration degree while being a stay-at-home father to his four beautiful children. He received his degree in 1995, but had a tough time finding suitable employment. Eventually he landed a position as a software analyst, where he still works today. This stability allowed him to come to terms with what had happened to him, what he had learned, and how he fit into this world.

Literary credits for David include the profile of his experience at the near-death. com website, his first book titled "Soul Bared: A Metaphysical Journey" and "Journey Through the World of Spirit: God, Gaia, and Guardian Angels."